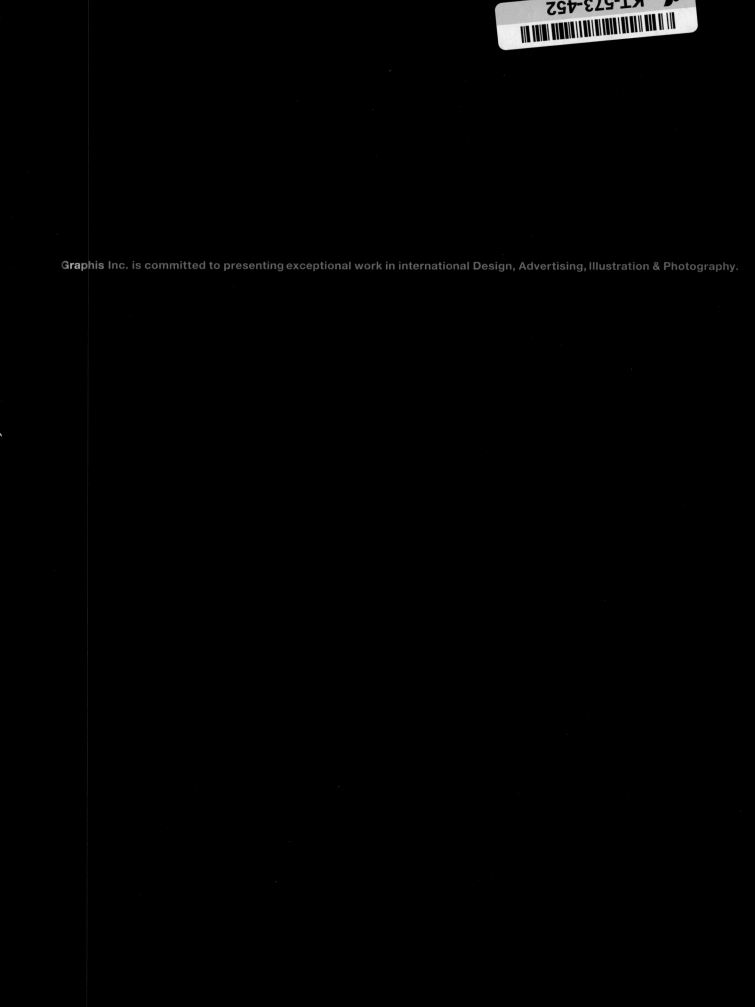

Graphis Inc. is committed to presenting exceptional work in international Design, Advertising, Illustration & Photography.

Published by Graphis | Publisher & Creative Director: B. Martin Pedersen | Design: Yon Joo Choi and Gregory Cerrato | Editorial: Abigail Lapp and Leah Michele Hansen | Production: Jennifer R. Berlingeri and Abigail Lapp | Webmaster: Abigail Lapp | Support Staff: Rita Jones | Design & Production Interns: Erica Banks, Danielle Leader, Guilet Libby, Tae Querney and Ping Yi Wang | Editorial Intern: Alison Zeidman

Remarks: We extend our heartfelt thanks to contributors throughout the world who have made it possible to publish a wide and international spectrum of the best work in this field. Entry instructions for all Graphis Books may be requested from: Graphis Inc., 307 Fifth Avenue, Tenth Floor, New York, New York 10016, or visit our web site at www.graphis.com.

Anmerkungen: Unser Dank gilt den Einsendern aus aller Welt. die es uns ermöglicht haben, ein breites, internationales. Spektrum der besten Arbeiten zu veröffentlichen. Teilnahmebedingungen für die Graphis-Bücher sind erhältlich bei: Graphis, Inc., 307 Fifth Avenue, Tenth Floor, New York, New York 10016. Besuchen Sie uns im World Wide Web, www.graphis.com.

Remerciements: Nous remercions les participants du monde entier qui ont rendu possible la publication de cet ouvrage offrant un panorama complet des meilleurs travaux. Les modalités d'inscription peuvent être obtenues auprès de: Graphis, Inc., 307 Fifth Avenue, Tenth Floor, New York, New York 10016. Rendez-nous visite sur notre site web: www.graphis.com.

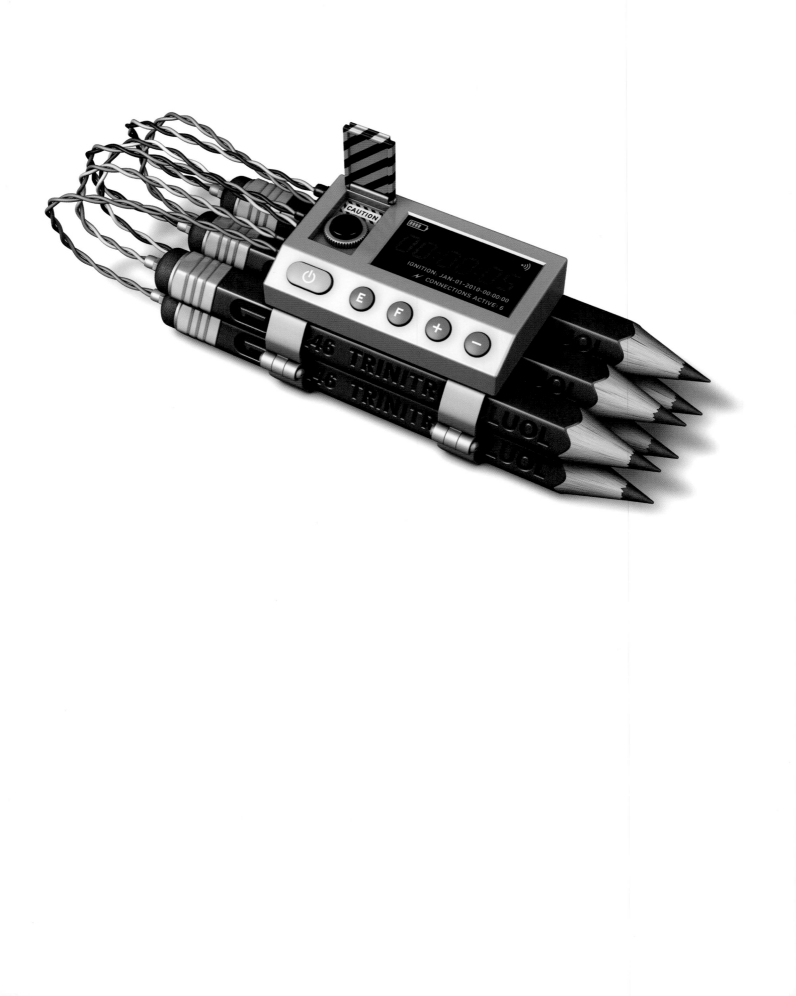

Contents

Previous spread: Image from AIGA Boston 25th Anniversary Book by Stoltze Design | *Opposite page:* Pencil Bomb by Peter Kraemer

InMemoriam

Hans Beck
Toy Designer
1929-2009

Kenneth Paul Block
Fashion Illustrator
1924-2009

Frank Cieciorka
Graphic Artist & Art Director
1939-2008

Heinz Edelmann
Designer & Art Designer
1934-2009

Bernie Fuchs
Illustrator
1932-2009

Lawrence Halprin
Landscape Architect
1916-2009

David Levine
Illustrator & Caricaturist
1926-2009

Noel Martin
Graphic Designer
1922-2009

Donal McLaughlin
Architect & Graphic Designer
1907-2009

Richard Merkin
Painter & Illustrator
1939-2009

Bob Noorda
Graphic Designer
1927-2010

Don Ivan Punchatz
Fantasy Illustrator
1936-2009

Jens Quistgaard
Industrial Designer
1919-2008

Viktor Schreckengost
Product Designer
1906-2008

Norman Schureman
Design & Illustration Professor
1959-2010

Tom Wilkes
Album Cover Designer
1939-2009

InMemoriam: David Levine

David Levine passed away in December 2009. A biting caricaturist who had more than 5,000 of his illustrations featured in such illustrious publications as Esquire, The New York Review of Books *and* Time, *he was also a gifted painter. The loss of his gentle scenes of Brooklyn life and intellectual, purposeful illustrations has left a hole that no illustrator or imitator could possibly hope to fill.*

Born in Brooklyn in 1926, David Levine grew up during the Golden Age of Comic Books. As a child, he was fascinated by newspaper comics, followed later by comic books. Levine's first artistic forays included copying drawings from Will Eisner's "The Spirit." In high school, he spent a good deal of time at the Brooklyn Museum, where its art school put the idea into his head to attend art school himself.

After serving a stint in the U.S. Army after World War II, Levine attended the Tyler School of the Arts at Temple University in Philadelphia. He earned degrees in education and art, then returned to New York amid the abstract expressionist movement. He enrolled in renowned painter Hans Hofman's school in Greenwich Village, where he experimented with abstract gestures. However, after a year he decided he preferred his earlier inspirations, painters Jean-Baptiste-Camille Corot, Pierre Bonnard, Jean-Édouard Vuillard and of course comic artist Will Eisner.

Levine continued to paint, but opted for smaller, realistic watercolors that featured scenes of people at work and play in Brooklyn, particularly beachgoers on Coney Island and garment workers, a tribute to the employees at his father's garment shop. Levine started drawing cartoons and illustrations in the 60s as a way to make money. His work first appeared in *Esquire* magazine in early 1958, and *The New York Review of Books* in 1963, where he would eventually contribute more than 3,800 portraits that defined the publication as much as its articles. Levine looked to draftsmen of the past for inspiration, including Thomas Nast, Honoré Daumier, Gustave Doré, Heinrich Kley, and Japanese masters Hokusai and Hiroshige. He worked from photographs and read the articles he was illustrating to get a true feel for the characters. The result was caricatures that did more than express a person's cartoon likeness, but rather distorted features into a personification of that subject's unique traits and behaviors.

Over the course of his career, Levine had thousands of his illustrations featured in various publications, and showed his paintings in several New York galleries. His caricatures lent an intellect and humor that has yet to be replicated, and his contribution to the tone of *The New York Review of Books* cannot be understated. His death is a true loss for erudite artistic pursuit.

(page 8) Passion at Coney, 1970; (page 9, top) Ramp to the Boardwalk; (page 9, bottom) Willam F. Buckley

Norman Mailer, Irwin Shaw, Max Roach, Alfred Kazin and thousands of other talented young people grew up believing that the longest journey of their lives would be the one across the Brooklyn Bridge. They all made that journey. So did David Levine.

Pete Hamill, *Writer (Graphis Issue 321: 1999)*

I might want to be critical, but I don't wish to be destructive. Caricature that goes too far simply lowers the viewer's response to a person as a human being.

David Levine, *from The New York Times,"David Levine, Biting Caricaturist, Dies at 83," Dec 29, 2009*

Heinz Edelmann, one of the world's greatest design talents, passed away in mid-2009. Best known for his art direction on The Beatles' "Yellow Submarine" film, he was also a prolific illustrator, graphic designer and advertiser, and was featured in Graphis magazine a dozen times.

Born in 1934 in Aussig in the former Czechoslovakia, Heinz Edelmann studied graphic arts at the State Academy of Art in Düsseldorf from 1953 to 1958. He then practiced freelance illustration and design, and in 1961 began teaching at the Düsseldorf school of applied art. He later taught at the Department of Applied Sciences Düsseldorf, the Fachhochschule Köln (Cologne factory schools) and the State Academy of Fine Arts in Stuttgart.

Edelmann's early illustration work for German magazine *Twen* is credited as setting a new trend in pop illustration in Germany. He is also widely regarded for his poster work, including several series for the West German Broadcasting Authority, the Westdeutscher Rundfunk radio station in Germany and the Düsseldorf theater company Kammerspiele, as well as myriad book covers and advertisements.

His career-defining work, Edelmann was the Art Director, Production Designer and Major Character Designer for The Beatles' psychedelic opus, "Yellow Submarine." The animated film featured bright, saturated colors and fanciful designs. Never one to be pigeonholed, Edelmann's later work was quite a departure from the film, taking on darker colors and more sinister-looking characters that lent themselves well to children's book illustration.

Throughout his career, Edelmann's penchant for self-renewal kept his work current, and a style that erred just on the other side of convention ensured that his designs stood out as distinctively his. Clever, whimsical and sometimes ironically dark, Heinz Edelmann's work maintains a wit that translates no matter the trend of the day. The design world won't be the same without him.

At the end of the year, I will hang up my pencil — not quite the dramatic gesture that hanging up one's gun, saber or even monkey wrench would be. The poor old 2B is going to look pretty ridiculous up there.

Heinz Edelmann, *Graphis Issue 340, 2002*

One of the most impressive things was that he was not only extremely well informed...but also that he was actually working in all the disciplines he talked about. Therefore his insights did not stem from some slowly grown academic wisdom and bitterness, but from his experience on a job finished just the night before.

Christoph Niemann, *Illustrator and former student (Graphis Issue 340, 2002)*

There is something unusual about [Heinz Edelmann's] work which often constitutes its charm. It is hardly surprising that he has a whole army of imitators, though their work can quickly be distinguished from his own originals.

Josef Rick, *former Head Officer, West German Broadcasting Authority (Graphis Issue 199, 1978)*

WESTFÄLISCHES MUSIKFEST
1986
9 8
GELSENKIRCHEN
30. MAI – 8. JUNI

VERANSTALTET VOM WESTDEUTSCHEN RUNDFUNK WDR UND DER STADT GELSENKIRCHEN

(page 10, first) The Patterned Night (By Brigitte Kronauer), 1981. Designer & Illustrator: Heinz Edelmann. Client: Klett-Cotta; (page 10, second) Further example of the quarterly posters listing children's television programmes, with full-color illustrations of their popular protagonists and of episodes from them.; (page 10, third) Poster announcing a programme series for young people with discussions of their problems.; (page 10, fourth) Das Geheimmis des Schönen Solange (By Vladimir Volkoff), 1990. Designer & Illustrator: Heinz Edelmann. Client: Klett-Cotta; (page 10, fifth) WDR Folk Festival, 1978. Designer & Illustrator: Heinz Edelmann, Client: WDR Westdeutscher Rundfunk; (page 11, top) Westfälisches Musikfest, 1984-1986. Designer, Illustrator & Creative Director: Heinz Edelmann, Client: WDR Westdeutscher Rundfunk; (page 11, bottom) Rattus Rex (By Colin McLaren). Collage, water-soluble grease-pencil, 1981. Designer & Illustrator: Heinz Edelmann, Client: Hobbit Presse / Klett-Cotta

What was the problem given when beginning this assignment?

Every year, Diageo produces a range of special release whiskies selected from very rare or now closed distilleries. This year, the premium spirits house introduced three more to its range: Mannochmore 18-Year Old, a boxed whisky produced in very limited quantities that retails for £200, Benrinnes 23-Year Old, and Pittyvaich 20-Year Old.

We were tasked with designing a look and feel consistent with the Special Releases range, but with a bespoke visual identity befitting of the character and the benefit of the distillery. The problem for the Mannochmore was to find the big idea for the brand based on the provenance and location of the distillery. The problem for the Benrinnes was to create a unique and distinctive identity for this limited edition whisky, building on its provenance and heritage. Also to create ownable elements such as the colour palette, typography and illustration style. The problem given for the Pittyvaich was to create a relevant and distinctive brand identity that would make it stand out from its competitive set.

The Single Cask range is a unique collection of 27 fine whiskies, selected from Diageo's distilleries and showcasing the variety of Diageo Scottish spirits. The range pulls together these vastly different whiskies in flavour and personality, each retaining their individuality and provenance, but married together under the mantle of "The Managers Choice." The problem was to align 27 different whiskies from 27 different distilleries whilst retaining an element of individual character.

Linkwood is a special release Speyside single malt scotch whisky, bottled at natural cask strength. Released as a range of three, each "flavour" is matured in either red wine, port or sherry casks. The task given was to find both structural packaging and a graphical livery for Linkwood, which, unusually, was to be sold in 50cl bottles. There was no existing identity so this had to be created.

How much direction did the client provide?

For Mannochmore, Diageo gave us an open brief to solve the problem in an original and compelling way, but within a given cost structure for its production. For Benrinnes, the client allowed us to come up with the ideas that reflected the brief of provenance, heritage and rarity. For Pittyvaich, as with the others, the client was very much part of the team and we worked at every stage together, but the final design was developed as our original visual with very little change to it.

For the Single Cask Selection, the client's only direction was that we had to unify the range with a single colour. We selected the Diageo maroon. For Linkwood, the client provided the story of the Linkwood history and of the distillery's family of swans, and we created the design around this.

How involved was the client in the design process?

With Mannochmore, the client is an expert in Scottish history and we worked with him in close consultation on every aspect of our design. With Benrinnes, the client worked with us at every stage as a partnership, helping us with the detailed historical background information and notes on the rarity of the whisky. The client is somebody that understands design and has a great respect for designers. Therefore, with Pittyvaich, besides a few details, we were left to do all the conceptual work independently.

With the Single Cask Selection, the client was involved in providing all mandatory on-pack information and got involved at the proofing and printing stages. For Linkwood, the client worked closely with us, providing all the information and support in making something quite different happen, appropriately for a different kind of product.

How did the rarity of these whiskies play into your designs?

For Mannochmore, the rarity was vital to the solution. Hand numbered bottles in limited editions importantly retained authenticity through the use of exact details, refined information and precious graphic presence. The rarity of the Benrinnes is key to its design. The typography on both bottle label and carton is reserved and describes the water source and terrain, allowing the 23-year old statement to stand out, therefore highlighting the rarity of age. The individual bottle and carton numbering is unique and enhances rarity. The rarity of Pittyvaich was of the utmost importance with individually numbered bottles highlighting this. The 20-year old is one of only 600 bottles.

The Managers Choice is a range of rare whiskies each coming from a single cask. Each bottle is uniquely numbered, as only a small number of bottles are produced, adding to their rarity and therefore value. Because

We were tasked with designing a look and feel consistent with the Special Releases range, but with a bespoke visual identity befitting of the character and the benefit of the distillery.

Mannochmore, Pittyvaich, Benrinnes and Linkwood have sold out, and early reports indicate that sales of the Single Cask Collection are outstripping demand.

of the limited quantities of the Linkwood, rarity was enhanced by the product being sold in atypical 50cl bottles. The precious typography, inspired by the distillery's original Germanic typeface and set in metal to give it authenticity, along with the hand-numbered bottles, helped communicate the product's rarity and authenticity.

How did you decide on the different bottle shapes? Do the shapes affect the whisky's flavor or character at all?

For the Mannochmore, the Benrinnes and the Pittyvaich, the bottles shapes were a "given" by the client, as this was felt to be the structure that best suited the whisky's character and allowed for elegant communication of the branding.

For the Single Cask Selection, the same bottle shape was chosen to create a unified classic look, the shape being perfect to show off each malt's colour in classic style. The bottle shape of the Linkwood reflected the elegance and sophistication of the whisky. The elongated bottle shows off the distinctive colours of the whisky and helps communicate their delicateness, especially as a 50cl format.

Birds play a role in the design of most of the bottles in this collection. Was this intentional? If so, how and why did you decide upon the bird motif?

On Mannochmore, the Greater Spotted Woodpecker is the region's native bird, which is constantly heard in the woods surrounding the distillery and therefore became the perfect symbol for Mannochmore, especially as we could link the 18 woodpecker holes to the 18 years of maturation the spirit undergoes in wood barrels. It was not intentional to use birds on all the Diageo whiskies, they are only used where relevant. There is no bird on Pittyvaich as it was not relevant, and we wanted to keep this packaging as an authentic piece of typography, enabling it to stand out.

The design for Benrinnes draws on the terrain of the area's beautiful heather-adorned landscape and endemic grouse bird. The heathery moorland and mountain water is a perfect environment for the grouse, therefore it became part of the illustration. There are 27 different symbols on the Single Cask Collection, each representing a distillery. Some distilleries, such as Glen Elgin, are represented by a bird; but others have boats, crests, compass, etc, each relevant as the distillery's unique and distinguishing mark.

A generations-old family of swans still live on the distillery pond and are therefore closely associated with Linkwood. Specially commissioned wood engravings of them were made.

How were the designs received by the client?

For Mannochmore, the client chose each design from three options but made the choice immediately, as he felt that the chosen design was exactly right for the brand of whisky. The client liked the bespoke wood engraving of the landscapes for Benrinnes and chose the design as his preferred choice on first sight of the visual. The client liked the very different look that the Pittyvaich packaging has, as it stood out from the competition, as the brief requested. A purely typographical look was achieved.

For the Single Cask Collection, the client proceeded to artwork with our first concept and was extremely pleased with the final outcome. We only produced one concept for Linkwood, which was accepted by the client even though it was quite unusual and broke the mould.

What were the sales results for the client?

Highly successful—Mannochmore, Pittyvaich, Benrinnes and Linkwood have sold out, and early reports indicate that sales of the Single Cask Collection are outstripping demand.

Where can these whiskies be purchased?

If at all, the whiskies can be purchased from specialist whisky shops such as London's Royal Mile Whiskies and Milroys, as well as from Diageo's "Friends of the Classic Malts."

The Brand Union: *The Brand Union is the leading global brand consultancy comprising world-class consultants, researchers and designers. The award-winning design house also currently holds the title of Design Agency of the Year, voted by Marketing magazine, UK. With 35 years of brand building heritage, The Brand Union's international footprint covers 18 major markets and offers brand expertise in research, strategy, design, engagement and communication services. The Brand Union is a WPP company.*

The Brand Union London:
11-33 St John Street, EC1M 4AA, United Kingdom
T: +44 (0) 20 7559 7000 / F: +44 (0) 20 7559 7001
www.thebrandunion.com

PlatinumWinners

pgs. 44-45 / Category: Books / Title: Kismet Yacht Book / Client: Kismet Yacht / Firm: pivot design, inc. / Designer: Jason Thompson / Executive Creative Director: Brock Haldeman

pgs. 46-47 / Category: Branding / Title: VONROSEN corporate design / Client: Von Rosen AG & Co. KG / Firm: KMS TEAM / Account Director: Katja Egloff / Art Director: Susana Frau / Creative Directors: Knut Maierhofer. Michael Keller / Designer: Teresa Lehmann

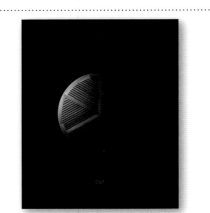

pgs. 76-77 / Category: Catalogues / Title: Nocturne Brochure / Client: David Sutherland, Inc. / Firm: David Sutherland. Inc. / Art Director: Melissa Englert / Creative Director: Tom Nynas / Photographers: Tom Nynas, John Wong, Ka Yeung

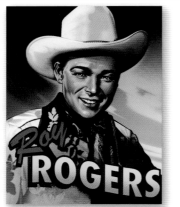

pg. 92 / Category: Designer Promotions / Title: A Lean Year / Client: Alt Group / Firm: Alt Group / Creative Director: Dean Poole / Designers: Aaron Edwards. Tony Proffit

pgs 134-135 / Category: Environment / Title: Madison Square Garden Presentation Center Interactive Experience / Client: Madison Square Garden / Firm: Hornall Anderson / See pages 240-241 for the complete credits

pg. 147 / Category: Illustration / Title: Cowboys of the Silver Screen / Client: United States Postal Service / Artist: Robert Rodriguez / Art Director: Carl T. Herrman

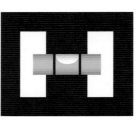

pg. 173 / Category: Logos / Title: Hanke Construction Logo / Client: Hanke Construction / Firm: TOKY Branding + Design / Creative Director: Eric Thoelke / Designer: Travis Brown

pgs. 192-197 / Category: Packaging / Titles: Mannochmore 18-year old; Linkwood 26-Year Old: The Managers Choice Single Cask Selection; Benrinnes 23-Year Old / Client: Diageo / Firm: The Brand Union / See page 245 for the complete credits

pg. 201 / Category: Posters / Title: "Another Japan" poster / Client: Japan Graphic Designers Association (JAGDA) / Firm: Ichiro Watanabe Graphics / Art Director, Designer: Ichiro Watanabe / Photographer: Toshiyuki Kuroishi

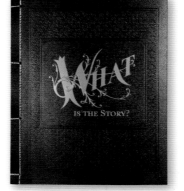

pgs. 218-219 / Category: Printer Promotion / Title: What is the Story? / Client: Fong & Fong Printers & Lithographers / Firm: ARGUS. LLC / Creative Director: Jeff Breidenbach / Designer: Stephanie Wade / Photographer: Sven Wiederholt

pg. 224 / Category: Stamps / Title: Mackinac Bridge (top), Bixby Bridge (bottom) / Client: U.S. Postal Service / Art Director: Carl T. Herrman / Artist: Dan Cosgrove

UP TOWN GIRL

This winter, explore tonal dressing in browns, from cream and caramel to chocolate and sepia. Coupling softness and strength, you can be the lady without giving up the girl.

Photography by Christopher Micaud
Style by Pascale Grisé

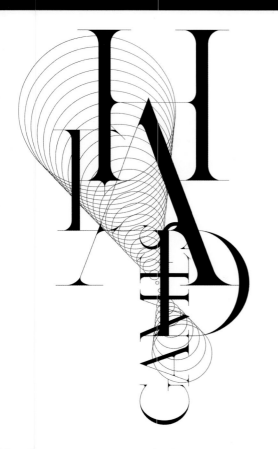

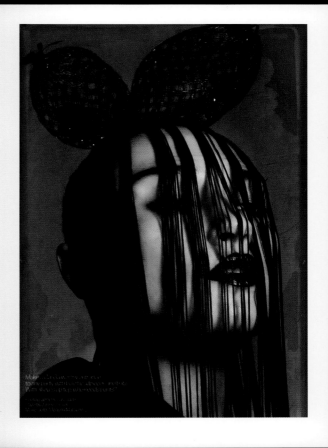

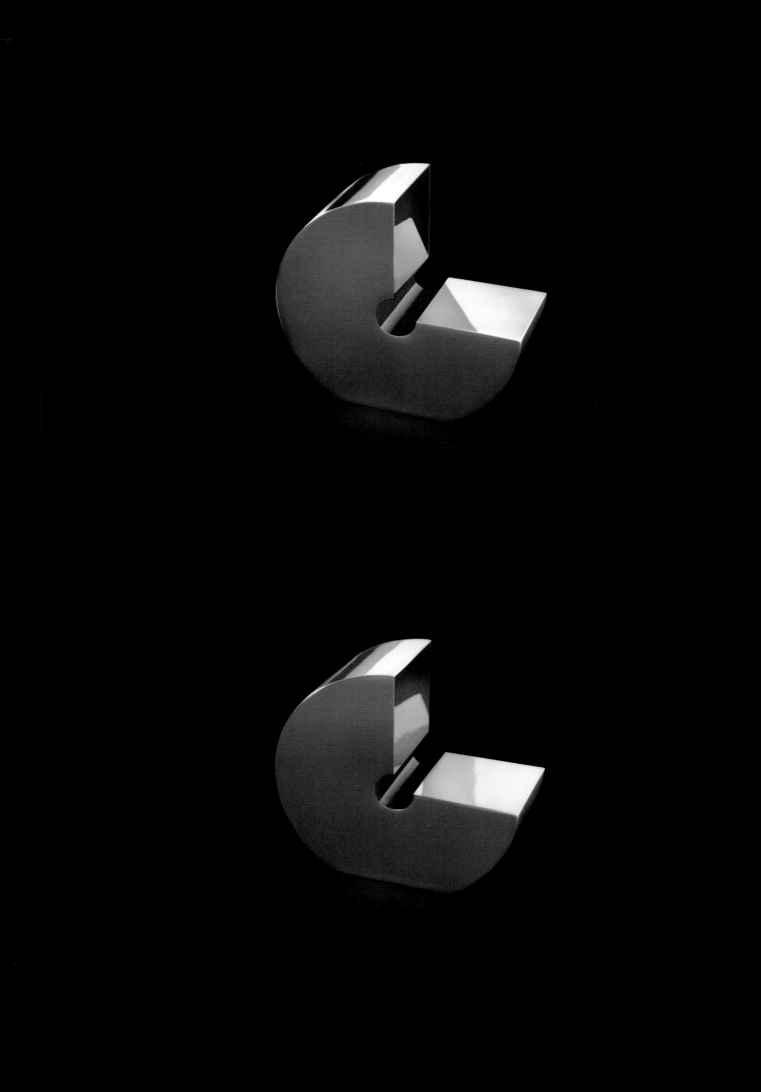

Award photograph by Henry Leutwyler

Graphis Platinum & Gold Award Winners by Location

The Americas

North America:

Canada	010
United States	153
Mexico	000

American Island Areas:

American Samoa	000
Guam	000
Northern Marianis	000
Palau	000
Puerto Rico	000
Virgin Islands	000

Caribbean:

Antigua and Barbuda	000
Bahamas	000
Barbados	000
Cayman Islands	000
Cuba	000
Dominica	000
Dominican Republic	000
Grenada	000
Haiti	000
Jamaica	000
St. Kitts and Nevis	000
St. Lucia	000
St. Vincent&The Grenadines	000
Trinidad&Tobago	000

Central America:

Belize	000
Costa Rica	000
El Salvador	000
Guatemala	000
Honduras	000
Nicaragua	000
Panama	000

South America:

Argentina	000
Bolivia	000
Brazil	001
Chile	000
Colombia	000
Ecuador	000
Guyana	000
Paraguay	000
Peru	000
Uruguay	000
Venezuela	000

Europe&Africa

Europe:

Northern Europe

Aland	000
Denmark	000
Faroe Islands	000
Finland	000
Greenland	000
Iceland	000
Karelia	000
Kola Peninsula	000
Norway	000
Sweden	000
Svalbard	000

Eastern Europe

Czech Republic	000
Hungary	000
Poland	000
Romania	000
Slovak Republic	000

Baltic States

Estonia	000
Latvia	000
Lithuania	000

Western Europe

Austria	001
Belgium	000
France	001
Germany	005
Ireland	000
Italy	000
Netherlands	001
Portugal	000
Spain	003
Switzerland	000
UK	015

Commonwealth of Independent States

Armenia	000
Azerbaijan	000
Belarus	000
Georgia	000
Kazakstan	000
Kyrgyzstan	000
Moldova	000
Russian Federation	000
Tajikistan	000
Turkmenistan	000
Ukraine	000
Uzbekistan	000

Southeast Europe

Albania	000
Bosnia-Herzegovina	000
Bulgaria	000
Croatia	001
Cyprus	000
Greece	000
Macedonia	000
Malta	000
Serbia&Montenegro	000
Slovenia	000
Turkey	000

Middle East:

Bahrain	000
Iran	000
Iraq	000
Israel / Occupied Territories	000
Jordan	000
Kuwait	000
Lebanon	000
Palestinian Authority	000
Saudi Arabia	000
Syria	000
UAE	000
Yemen	000

Africa:

North Africa

Algeria	000
Egypt	000
Libya	000
Morocco West Sahara	000
Tunisia	000

Central Africa

Burundi	000
Cameroon	000
Cent. African Rep.	000
Chad	000
Congo	000
DR Congo	000

Equatorial Guinea	000
Rwanda	000

Southern Africa

Angola	000
Malawi	000
Mozambique	000
Namibia	000
South Africa	000
Swaziland	000
Zambia	000
Zimbabwe	000

East Africa

Eritrea	000
Ethiopia	000
Kenya	000
Somalia	000
Sudan	000
Tanzania	000
Uganda	000

West Africa

Burkina Faso	000
Cote D'Ivoire	000
Ghana	000
Guinea	000
Guinea-Bissau	000
Liberia	000
Mauritania	000
Niger	000
Nigeria	000
Senegal	000
Sierra Leone	000
Togo	000

Asia&Oceania

Asia:

East Asia

China	005
Japan	002
Mongolia	000
North Korea	000
South Korea	001
Taiwan	000

Southwest Asia

Brunei Darussalam	000
Cambodia	000
Indonesia	000
Laos	000
Malaysia	000
Myanmar	000
Philippines	000
Singapore	000
Thailand	000
Timor-Leste	000
Viet Nam	000

South Asia

Afghanistan	000
Bangladesh	000
Bhutan	000
India	000
Maldives	000
Nepal	000
Pakistan	000
Sri Lanka	000

Oceania:

Australia	005
Fiji	000
New Zealand	005
Papua New Guinea	000
Solomon Islands	000

Total Winning Entries **209**

Mineta San Jose International Airport
San Jose, California, USA

Gensler

Shift

Annual Report 2009

Reed Smith
London, England, UK

T-Mobile Creation Center
Seattle, Washington, USA

75 YEARS OF
RESOLVING LABOR-
MANAGEMENT DISPUTES

1934 – 2009

NATIONAL MEDIATION BOARD
ANNUAL PERFORMANCE AND
ACCOUNTABILITY REPORT FY 2009

NMB75

**ALTERNATIVE
DISPUTE
RESOLUTION**

During fiscal year 2009, members of the Office of
Alternative Dispute Resolution Services engaged
in direct delivery of dispute resolution services as
facilitators in grievance mediation, as facilitators
in interest-based contract negotiations, and as
trainers in a variety of programs. Internally, across
all departments, ADRS provided consultant
services by developing and otherwise assisting
in business process improvement and helping
to create innovative approaches to fulfilling the
NMB's goals and statutory obligations.

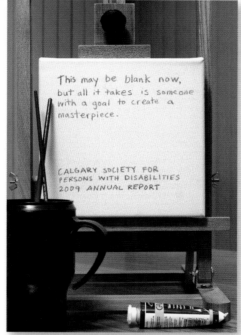

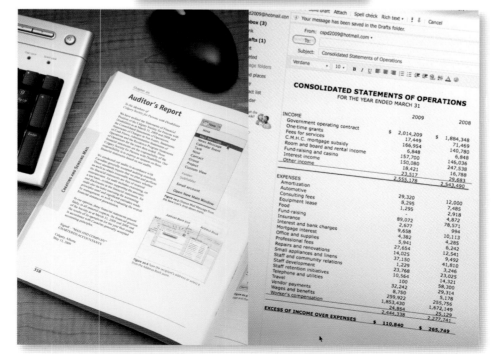

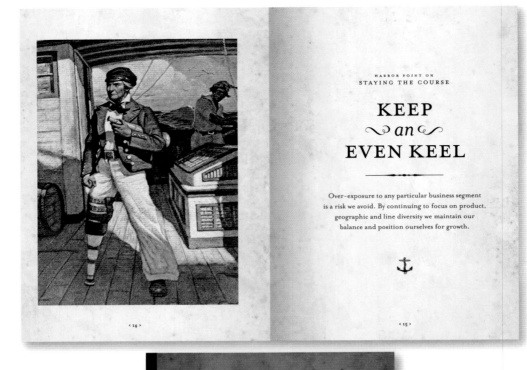

KEEP
~an~
EVEN KEEL

Over-exposure to any particular business segment is a risk we avoid. By continuing to focus on product, geographic and line diversity we maintain our balance and position ourselves for growth.

⚓

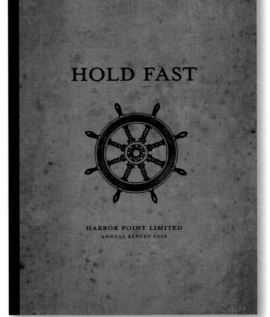

HOLD FAST

HARBOR POINT LIMITED
ANNUAL REPORT 2008

HARBOR POINT LIMITED
FINANCIAL HIGHLIGHTS

GROSS WRITTEN PREMIUMS

2008	$511,714
2007	$672,476
2006	$642,610

SHAREHOLDERS' EQUITY

2008	$1,691,472
2007	$1,578,992
2006	$1,461,932

OPERATING INCOME

2008	$64,053
2007	$170,106
2006	$84,585

COMBINED RATIO

Year	Value
2008	103.2%
2007	86.0%
2006	92.8%

HARBOR POINT LIMITED
FINANCIAL HIGHLIGHTS

For the years ended and as of December 31, 2008, 2007 and 2006 (Expressed in thousands of U.S. dollars)

	2008	2007	2006
INCOME STATEMENT HIGHLIGHTS			
Gross premiums written	$ 511,714	$ 672,476	$ 642,610
Net premiums earned	519,210	532,156	299,188
Net investment income	95,311	98,310	68,666
Operating income	64,053	170,106	84,585
Operating return on equity	4.3%	10.8%	6.0%
UNDERWRITING RATIOS			
Loss ratio	69.9%	47.3%	43.7%
Expense ratio	33.3%	38.7%	49.1%
Combined ratio	103.2%	86.0%	92.8%
BALANCE SHEET HIGHLIGHTS			
Invested assets	$2,232,068	$2,036,692	$1,557,932
Shareholders' equity	1,691,472	1,578,992	1,461,932
FINANCIAL STRENGTH RATINGS			
A.M. Best	A (Excellent)		
Standard & Poor's	A- (Strong)		

1983
Membership Promotion
DESIGN AND PHOTOGRAPHY: Skolos-Wedell

1984
Lecture Announcement
DESIGN AND PHOTOGRAPHY: Skolos-Wedell

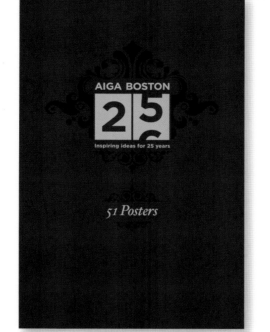

AIGA BOSTON

2 5

Inspiring ideas for 25 years

51 Posters

1989
Lecture Series Announcement
DESIGN: Stoltze Design

1990
Exhibit Announcement
DESIGN: Quorum

Bill Walton Catalog
Designlore

ART DIRECTOR Laurie Churchman **DESIGNERS** Frank Baseman, Todd Vachon **PHOTOGRAPHERS** Bill Walton, Jane Irish, Dan Husted + others **WRITERS** Richard Torchia, Christopher Youngs, Eileen Neff, Susan Rosenberg, Judith Tannenbaum, Patrick T Murphy **CLIENT** Arcadia University

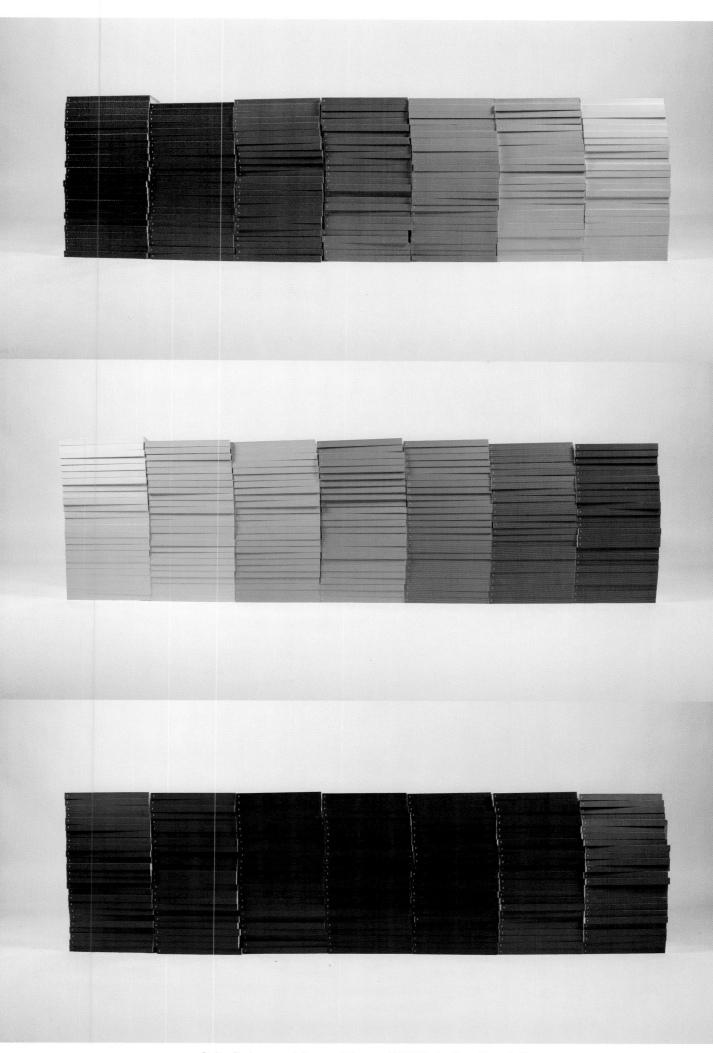

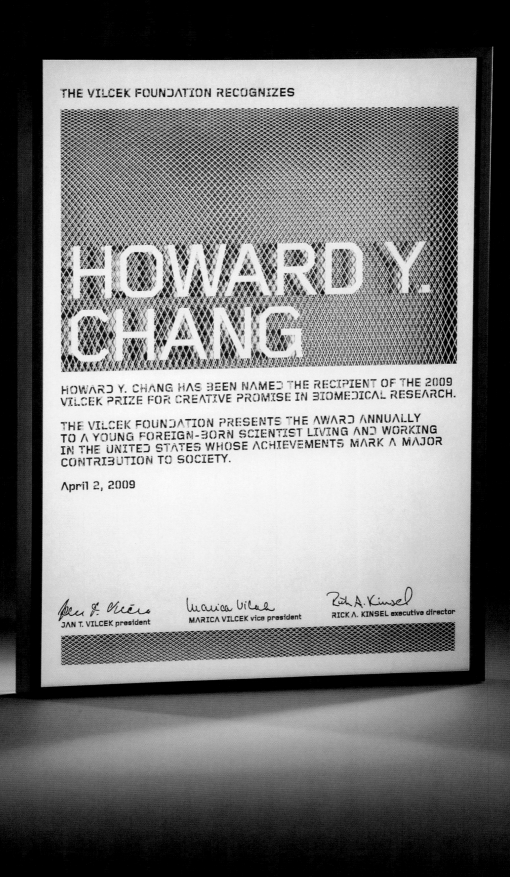

HAM TRAN HAS BEEN NAMED THE RECIPIENT OF THE 2006 VILCEK PRIZE FOR CREATIVE PROMISE IN FILMMAKING. THE VILCEK FOUNDATION PRESENTS THE AWARD ANNUALLY TO A YOUNG FOREIGN-BORN ARTIST LIVING AND WORKING IN THE UNITED STATES WHOSE ACHIEVEMENTS MARK A CONTRIBUTION TO SOCIETY.

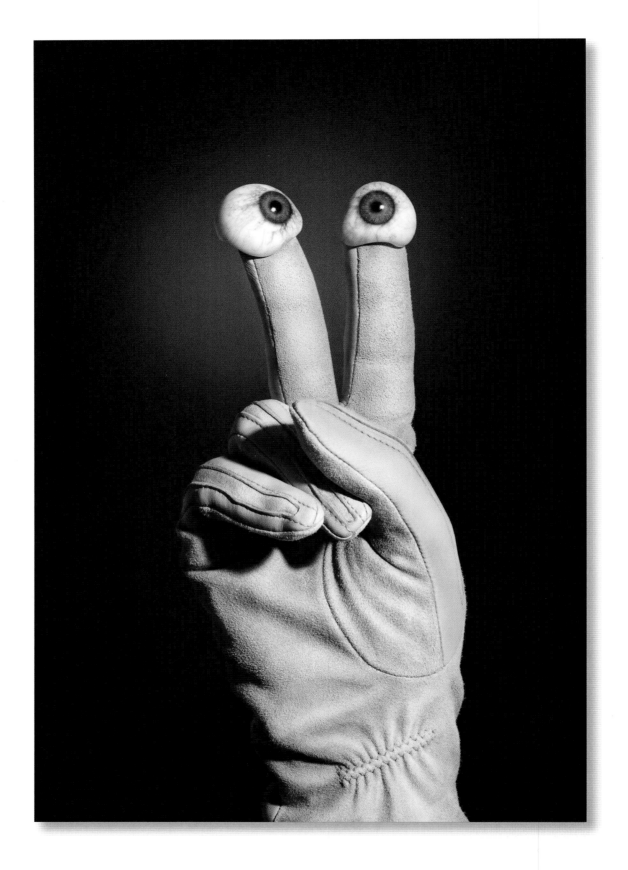

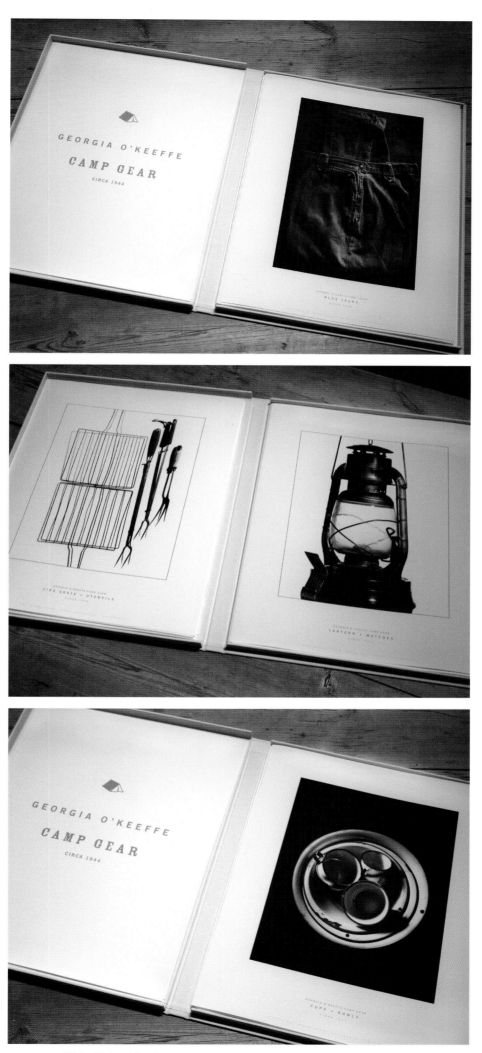

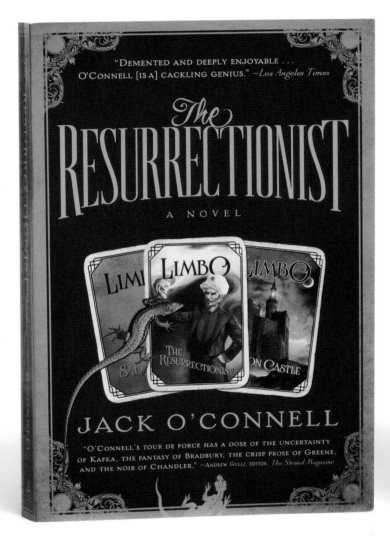

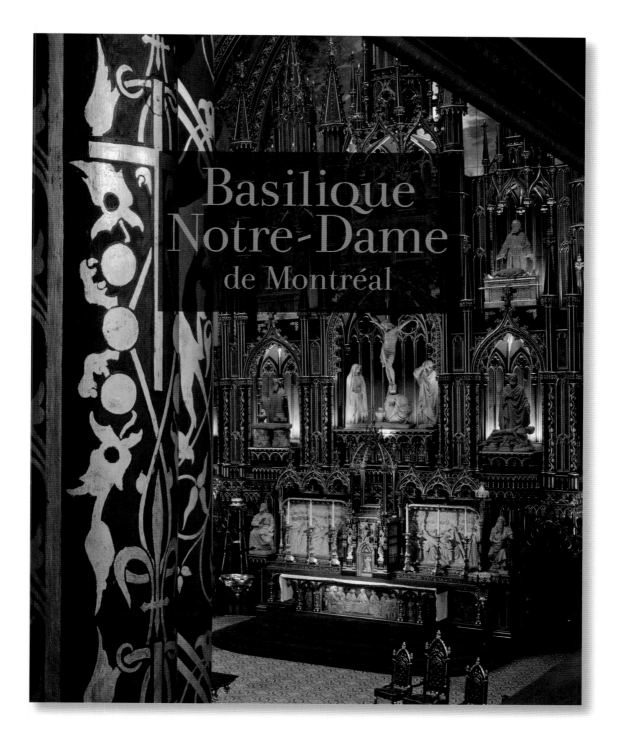

Basilique
Notre-Dame
de Montréal

Augusten Burroughs

YOU BETTER NOT CRY

Stories for Christmas

#1 *New York Times* Bestselling Author of *Running With Scissors*

courage

alan littell

a novel

"From the classic tropes of the detective procedural, this debut novel weaves the kind of mannered fantasy that might result if Wes Anderson were to adapt Kafka."
—*The New Yorker*

The Manual of Detection

a novel

JEDEDIAH BERRY

A THREAD OF SKY

A NOVEL

DEANNA FEI

THERE ONCE LIVED A WOMAN WHO TRIED TO KILL HER NEIGHBOR'S BABY

SCARY FAIRY TALES

LUDMILLA PETRUSHEVSKAYA

KEITH GESSEN

ANNA SUMMERS

St. Martin's Press www.stmartins.com (top left) | St. Martin's Press
Penguin Group (USA) Inc. www.us.penguingroup.com (top right, bottom) | Penguin Group (USA) Inc. | Books 37

C. S. Lewis

MERE
CHRISTIANITY

—

C. S. Lewis

MIRACLES

—

C. S. Lewis

The
PROBLEM
OF PAIN

—

C. S. Lewis

GEORGE
MACDONALD

—

DARWIN'S ARMADA

Four Voyages and the Battle for the Theory of Evolution

•• IAIN McCALMAN ••

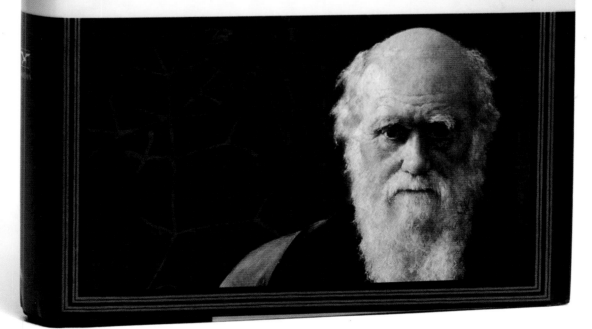

MODEL AS MUSE

MEG MUNDY, MARILYN AMBROSE, HELEN BENNETT, DANA JENNEY, BETTY McLAUCHLEN, LISA FONSSAGRIVES, LILY CARLSON, DORIAN LEIGH, ANDREA JOHNSON, ELIZABETH GIBBONS, KAY HERNAN, MURIEL MAXWELL, IRVING PENN (TRAINA-NORELL, CLAIRE McCARDELL, NETTIE ROSENSTEIN, HATTIE CARNEGIE, CEIL CHAPMAN, MARK MOORING, CHARLES JAMES

RENE RUSSO | PATRICK DEMARCHELIER | CHRISTIAN DIOR

Acknowledgments | Exhibition Checklist | Bibliography | Photograph Credits

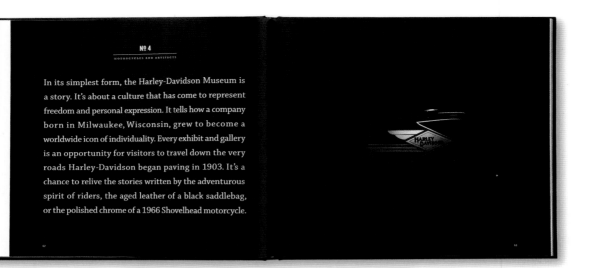

In its simplest form, the Harley-Davidson Museum is a story. It's about a culture that has come to represent freedom and personal expression. It tells how a company born in Milwaukee, Wisconsin, grew to become a worldwide icon of individuality. Every exhibit and gallery is an opportunity for visitors to travel down the very roads Harley-Davidson began paving in 1903. It's a chance to relive the stories written by the adventurous spirit of riders, the aged leather of a black saddlebag, or the polished chrome of a 1966 Shovelhead motorcycle.

CONTENTS

Bridge connecting the Museum to Motor restaurant and The Shop.

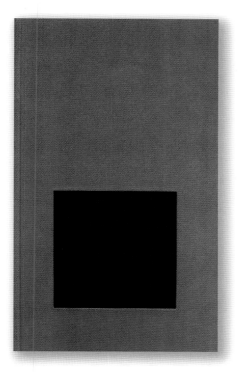

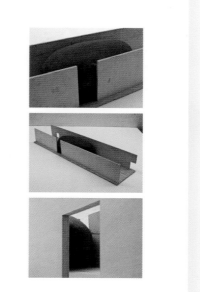

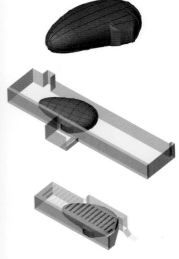

Model for *Memory*, mock-up for Deutsche Guggenheim gallery.

Above: Computer-generated image of final form for *Memory*. Center: Computer-generated image of *Memory* installed at Deutsche Guggenheim, Berlin. Below: Computer-generated image of *Memory* installed at Solomon R. Guggenheim Museum, New York.

murmur, "but the paint here is not getting really pushed around by that cutting edge." Ah, but representation, even when only of an analogical abstraction, tracing, is a losing battle. Or is the artist playing to lose? Unknowable. The most striking thing when Kapoor speaks is his humility. "I am interested in the old questions that I cannot answer." Catch the trace is the oldest problem in the book.

Just after I had my first walk through Kapoor's studio in February 2008, I spoke to a group in Austria and said something like this: Just descriptively, upstream from politics, globalization is an island of languaging in a field of traces. What, then, is a trace? A sign system promises meaning. A trace does not promise anything. It is something that seems to suggest that there was something before. Think of the world's richness of languages, and then think of what happens with the visual. I myself began to think of this much more carefully when I was with Kapoor three or four weeks ago. He is making a colossal sculpture for the Deutsche Guggenheim and I was asked to write an essay about it. As I'm trying to figure out what it is that this very smart guy wants, I am beginning to realize that he is trying to represent *traces* (*Zwischenräume der Zeit*).[3] That's not a sign system; it's like a *Spur* (the German word for trace). It's like seeing elephant shit on the forest floor. It can be either that there were elephants, or, it could be that you are hallucinating. Or it could be that someone put the excrement there as a decoy. It is an indefinite "inventory of traces." A trace is not a sign. Rather than theorize globalization as a general field of translation which (in spite of all the empiricization of apparently impersonal, mechanical translation,) privileges host or target, we should instead learn to think that the human subject in globalization is an island of languaging—unevenly understanding some languages and idioms with the "first" language as a monitor—within an entire field of traces where understanding follows no guarantee.

If, then, for me, looking at Kapoor's work, globalization became supplemented as an island of language in an ocean of traces. I have to go back to the binary opposition of verbal and visual denied by this intuition: namely, that art is visual, not verbal; that "language" can be used here only metaphorically. Then the question of truth in the visual, implicated in all non-expressive art, perhaps in all art, looms. And what might a trace be, in this understanding of globalization opened up for me by a walk through Kapoor's studio? To repeat: globalization makes us live on an island of language in an ocean of traces, with uncertain shores ever on the move. This "us" extends all the way to the unending circulation of labor exported from the global South. Each member or collectivity belonging to this tremendously large group understands one or a few languages and is sure that the other organizations of noise are meaning-full but not for him or her. Language and trace are here in a gender-differentiated taxonomy, rather than merely opposed (*Her Blood*, 1998). The presence of women in migrancy is class-differentiated, differentiated by their differential hold over and access to language and languages.

Why did I get this sense of globalization in Kapoor's studio? Let us approach this question stealthily and indirectly. Let us say that language is a system that promises verifiable conceptual meaning. Everybody knows that the performance of a language is full of mystery, but the promise of meaning is always there. A trace, by contrast, seems to suggest an anteriority of some sort, altogether unverifiable. The thin figure of the trace lurks in the crannies of nuanced human endeavor. I have suggested elsewhere that Immanuel Kant's philosophy of pure reason may be a "management of the undermining risk of the trace." Jacques Derrida suggested in 1968 that the thought of the trace can curb the universalizing arrogance of language: "I have attempted to indicate a way out of the closure of this framework via the 'trace,' which is no more an effect than it has a cause, but which in and of itself, without extra-textual gloss [*hors texte*], is not sufficient to operate the necessary transgression." The universalizing ambition of globalization would here qualify as a species of transgression, and Derrida feels that the thought of the trace might curb in the epistemic sphere. And the curb might work as a solution in the field of the vanity of human wishes held up by capital. In a certain sense the non-verbal visual always traffics in traces. In another sense it is ever tempted, in its allegorical reaches

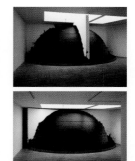

Past, Present, Future, 2006. Wax and oil-based paint, 45 x 890 x 445 cm. Installation: Lisson Gallery, London.

50

VONROSEN

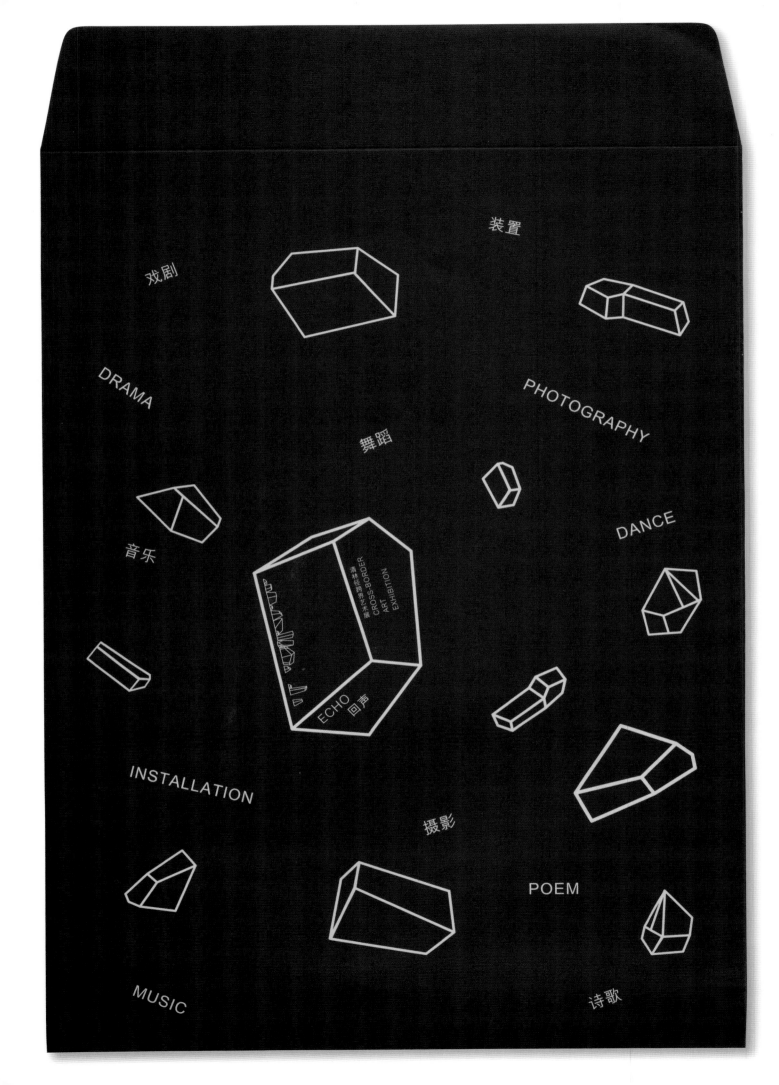

装置

戏剧

DRAMA

PHOTOGRAPHY

舞蹈

音乐

DANCE

清林桂跨界艺术展 CROSS-BORDER ART EXHIBITION

ECHO 回声

INSTALLATION

摄影

POEM

MUSIC

诗歌

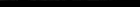

Smarter Energy

Smarter Oil

Smarter Public Safety

Smarter Communication

Smarter Water

Smarter Education

Smarter Cities

Smarter Work

THINK

Perspective

Innovation beyond current convention.

Design is our soul.

It defines our purpose. It inspires our process. It sustains our passion.

The core of every project...
every new opportunity...
every emergent idea is design.

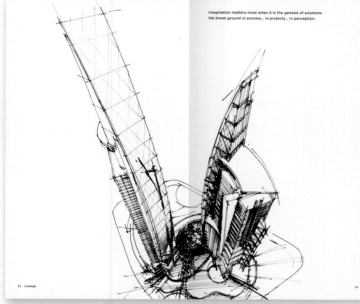

Imagination matters most when it is the genesis of solutions.
We break ground in process... in projects... in perception.

Projects

There is nothing we are more passionate about than design.

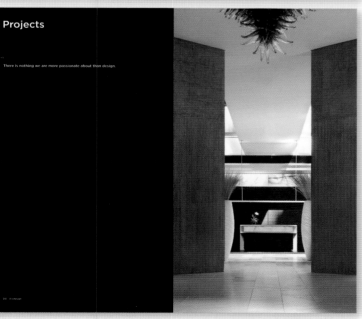

We are tvsdesign.

tvs-design.com

Passionate about
design excellence.
Innovative.
Collaborative.
Insightful.

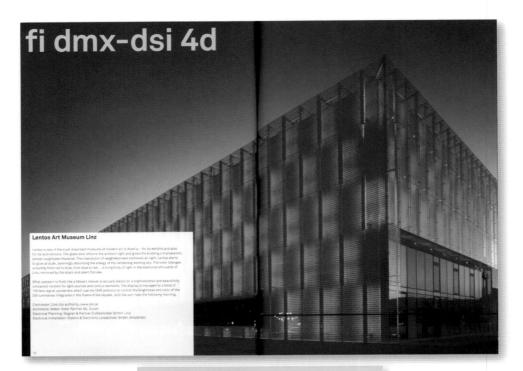

fi dmx-dsi 4d

Lentos Art Museum Linz

Lentos is one of the most important museums of modern art in Austria – for its exhibits and also for its architecture. The glass skin reflects the ambient light and gives the building a transparent, almost weightless character. This impression of weightlessness continues at night. Lentos starts to glow at dusk, seemingly absorbing the energy of the reddening evening sky. The color changes smoothly from red to blue, from blue to red ... a living body of light in the nocturnal silhouette of Linz, mirrored by the black and silent Danube.

What appears to float like a Mozart minuet is actually based on a sophisticated and beautifully conceived recipe for light sources and control elements. The display is managed by a total of 116 feno signal converters which use the DMX protocol to control the brightness and color of the DSI luminaires integrated in the frame of the facade, until the sun rises the following morning.

Contractor: Linz city authority, www.linz.at
Architects: Weber Hofer Partner AG, Zurich
Electrical Planning: Wagner & Partner Ziviltechniker GmbH, Linz
Electrical Installation: Elektro & Electronic Landsteiner GmbH, Amstetten

12

feno before light and beyond

fi pwm-analog 4d

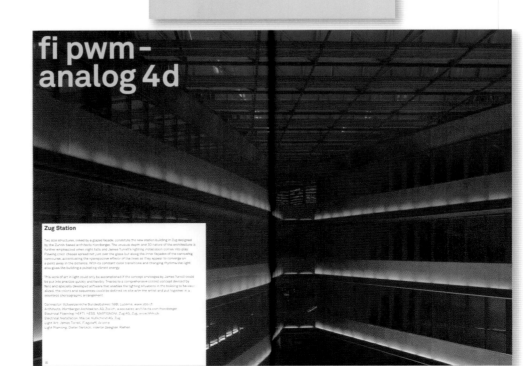

Zug Station

Two slim structures, linked by a glazed facade, constitute the new station building in Zug designed by the Zurich-based architects Hornberger. The unusual depth and 3D nature of the architecture is further emphasized when night falls and James Turrell's lighting installation comes into play. Flowing color phases spread not just over the glass but along the inner facades of the narrowing concourse, accentuating the «perspective effect» of the lines as they appear to converge on a point away in the distance. With its constant color transitions and changing rhythms the light also gives the building a pulsating vibrant energy.

This work of art in light could only be accomplished if the concept envisaged by James Turrell could be put into practice quickly and flexibly. Thanks to a comprehensive control concept devised by feno and specially developed software that enables the lighting situations in the building to be visualized, the colors and sequences could be defined on site with the artist and put together in a seamless choreographic arrangement.

Contractor: Schweizerische Bundesbahnen SBB, Lucerne, www.sbb.ch
Architects: Hornberger Architekten AG, Zurich, www.swiss-architects.com/hornberger
Electrical Planning: HEFTI, HESS, MARTIGNONI Zug AG, Zug, www.hhm.ch
Electrical Installation: Macus Hufschmid AG, Zug
Light Art: James Turrell, Flagstaff, Arizona
Light Planning: Dieter Bartsch, Interior Designer, Riehen

16

このイニシアチブは、アジア諸国の政策研究機関が世界各国の政策研究機関と連携する能力を高め、平和と安全保障を促進する新構想の策定を支援します。

アジア諸国の経済・政治力の高まりに伴い、世界構造に変化がもたらされています。今後数十年にわたり、アジア太平洋は世界経済を牽引し、この地域に新たな繁栄をもたらすことになるでしょう。それと同時に、大国間の対立、資源不足といった、安全保障上の問題により、この地域の発展が後退する可能性もあります。この地域の変化に合わせ、アジア太平洋地域は、平和と繁栄のための新たな連携のあり方を模索する必要があるのです。

ジョン＆キャサリン・マッカーサー財団は、アジアでの平和と安全保障を確立する最善の方法は地域協力を通じてであると考え、7年間にわたり6,800万ドルの基金を新アジア安全保障イニシアチブに投じています。このイニシアチブは、アジア諸国の政策研究機関が世界各国の政策研究機関と連携する能力を高め、平和と安全保障促進へ向けた新構想を策定する援助をします。また同イニシアチブは、新しい中堅キャリア層フェローシップ・プログラムとして、アジア安全保障新興指導者プログラムを助成します。このプログラムでは、将来的な安全保障問題の克服にむけて協調できる新しい世代の指導者を育成します。

アジア安全保障問題：なぜ、今アジアなのか？

世界人口70億の半分以上が住むアジア。ますます高まるこの地域の経済力、政治力は、地域を変えつつあります。中国・インド両国の経済は、2050年までに米国経済の規模を抜くと予想されています。現在、世界の国内総生産（GDP）の半分以上を抜きアジア太平洋諸国が占めています。アジア太平洋社会全体で実現した世界を変革する技術革新により、アップル社製 iPod に搭載されるマイクロチップは、アメリカやインドでプログラミング後、台湾で製造、韓国でテストを経て、中国で装着されます。

経済面での協調と貿易関係が深まる一方で、国家間紛争が複雑な安全保障問題を生み出し、アジア地域の繁栄の存続を脅かしています。韓国のソウルは、世界で最も活気あふれる都市の一つとされ、フォーチュン500社のうち11社がここに本社をかまえています。しかし、わずか30マイル離れたところでは、狭い武装地帯が北朝鮮武装軍（100万）と、韓国軍（60万）・米国軍（3万）を隔てています。朝鮮半島、その他アジア太平洋諸国の多くの紛争の火種を抱える地域での衝突回避を目的に、アジア太平洋諸国政府がどのように協調していくか。これが、アジア地域人口35億人が今後も平和と繁栄の恩恵を享受できるか否かの鍵を握っています。

次々に変化する国家同士の関係に慎重な対処が要求されているのに加え、アジア諸国の自国民の安全保障能力に対する更なる試練となっているのが、国境を超えた問題です。たとえば、ベトナム、カンボジア、バングラデシュ、中国の東南アジア各国にとり、メコン川は農業・商業・移動の生命線です。それにもかかわらず、水資源の需要が増大した地域において、それら資源へのアクセスを管理する法制、地域機構、政策の開発が不十分です。このような問題に国・地域レベルで建設的に対応することで、紛争の回避を助け、それにより同地域の安定と安全保障の促進につながるのです。

11

The John D. and Catherine T. MacArthur Foundation

亚洲国家不断增强的经济和政治实力正在改变世界。亚太地区将在未来几十年内充当世界经济的引擎，这将帮助区域内数以百万计的人口获得繁荣。与此同时，区域正在面临着安全的挑战——从大国冲突到资源的匮乏，这些挑战如果无法得到合理的化解，将大大损害区域的经济与社会成就。当亚太区域开始转变的时候，区域内的不同社会需要找到新的方法，为了和平与繁荣的利益合作共进。

由于认识到实现亚洲和平与安全的最佳途径是地区合作，麦克阿瑟基金会（John D. and Catherine T. MacArthur Foundation）将在未来 7 年内向一项新的"亚洲安全倡议"（Asia Security Initiative, 简称PSI）投资6800 万美元。此项倡议将帮助亚洲的政策研究机构加强与全球同行进行合作的能力，为亚洲的和平与安全事业出谋划策。此外，基金会还将支持一项新的在职培训工作计划，即"亚洲安全新兴领导人计划"（Asia Security Emerging Leaders Program），它旨在培养致力于通过合作克服未来安全挑战的新一代领导人。

亚洲安全挑战：为什么是亚洲，为什么是现在？

亚洲拥有全球 70 亿人中一半以上的人口，其不断增强的经济和政治实力正日益改变着世界。中国和印度的经济总量有望到 2050 年超过美国，环太平洋国家的经济总量现已占到全球国民生产总额的一半以上。亚太地区已经取得了全球日新月异的技术创新。例如，每一台"苹果"iPod 电脑赖以运行的微芯片是美国的产品，但由印度负责编程、台湾负责生产、韩国负责测试和中国负责安装。

尽管国家间的经济合作与贸易关系不断加深，但国与国之间不断发展的争议也在引发复杂的安全挑战，威胁到亚太地区经济繁荣的延续。全球财富 500 强企业中已有 11 家把总部设在了全球最富活力的城市之一——韩国首尔。然而，距首尔仅 30 英里处便是一条狭窄的"非军事区"。"非军事区"的两边，一边驻扎着全副武装的 100 万朝鲜军队，另一边扎着 60 万韩国军队和 3 万美国军队。为防止在朝鲜半岛、以及其他存在着冲突隐患的亚太地区的冲突升级，亚太地区中的各国政府如何展开合作，决定着该地区38亿人口能否继续享有和平与繁荣带来的种种益处。

当亚洲国家不断着手调整国家与国家关系的同时，跨国问题也在不断挑战着各国为本国国民提供安全的能力。例如，东南亚的湄公河对于越南、柬埔寨、孟加拉国和中国的农业、商业与旅游业来说，都是一条极为重要的生命线。然而，在这样一个对水资源需求不断增长的时代，用于管理水资源使用权所需的相关制度、地区机制和政策却十分滞后。面对此类挑战，国家和区域如能做出建设性的回应，将有助于避免冲突，进而促进区域的稳定和安全。

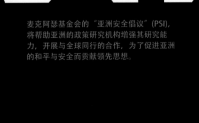

麦克阿瑟基金会的"亚洲安全倡议"(PSI)，将帮助亚洲的政策研究机构增强其研究能力，开展与全球同行的合作，为了促进亚洲的和平与安全而贡献领先思想。

6

7

STYLE THAT MOVES YOUR SENSES—AND YOUR SOUL.

REFINED

STRENGTH

KIZASHI GTS
Shown in Platinum Silver Metallic

SUZUKI 2010

KIZASHI

CHURNS UP A SUBLIME, BEST-IN-CLASS 185 HORSEPOWER AND...

POWERFUL

EXCITEMENT

KIZASHI GTS
Shown in Vivid Red

KIZASHI GTS
Shown in Platinum Silver Metallic

KIZASHI SLS
Shown in Black interior

iPod MENU
PLAY LIST

KIZASHI GTS
Shown in Platinum Silver Metallic

LUX

#1
September
October
November
2008

A Season To See.

FROM THE DIRECTOR

April marked Lux's first decade, and we have accomplished much. We found a perfectly suited four-and-a-half acre site on which to create the Lux campus, completed the first phase of our facilities, and surrounded it with a unique, native landscape. We opened its doors ago and are heating up to see visitors at work, sharing with them the creative process—as it happens.

By opening the doors of the artist's studio and making public what has traditionally been a private act, our visitors engage with the artistic process and watch a masterpiece evolve.

Now, we are preparing to launch our second season of artist residencies, bringing you some of the most inventive and interesting artists of our time—at work in the studio. We invite you to share their journey of invention and watch with us as ideas in the artist's mind take physical form. Visit Lux, watch art happen, and experience the museum, redefined.

Reeny Shaw

Ray Smith
IN STUDIO
SEPTEMBER 12, 2008
through
SEPTEMBER 27, 2008
ON EXHIBIT
SEPTEMBER 12, 2008
through
NOVEMBER 1, 2008

Alison Moritsugu
IN STUDIO
NOVEMBER 8, 2008
through
DECEMBER 6, 2008
ON EXHIBIT
NOVEMBER 8, 2008
through
JANUARY 3, 2009

Jolynn Krystosek
IN STUDIO
JANUARY 10, 2009
through
JANUARY 31, 2009
ON EXHIBIT
JANUARY 10, 2009
through
MARCH 18, 2009

Victoria Adams
IN STUDIO
MARCH 28, 2009
through
APRIL 4, 2009
ON EXHIBIT
MARCH 28, 2009
through
MAY 30, 2009

Derrick Guild
IN STUDIO
MAY 28, 2009
through
JUNE 20, 2009
ON EXHIBIT
MAY 28, 2009
through
AUGUST 1, 2009

Cover: Ray Smith, Perrito (detail), 1997. Oil on canvas, 35 x 135 cm. Collection of Matratxi and Ray Smith.

Last November, Lux opened its doors—and the artistic process—to the public with an exciting new artist-in-residence program. This fall, Lux builds on the first year's success with an equally engaging and diverse lineup of artists for the 2008–2009 season. Some follow more traditional genres, such as landscape or surrealist painting. Others turn these traditions on their head, or find new mediums in which to work.

New York painter and sculptor Ray Smith kicks off our second season September 12. Born in Texas and raised in Mexico City, Smith's surrealistic works often feature dogs and animals as surrogates, shamans, or symbols of the more primal nature of man lurking beneath the surface.

Alison Moritsugu is Lux's second artist of the season. Born in Hawaii but based in New York, Moritsugu is best known for her series of Luminist landscapes painted on log slices. These works frame nature in fresh ways and call attention to our complex relationship with the environment.

New York-based artist Jolynn Krystosek opens the New Year at Lux with her wax floral relief carvings, drawings of exotic fowl and large-scale, site-specific paper cut-outs. Although very different mediums, Krystosek uses each to examine ideas of vitality, decay and seduction, and encourage viewers to reflect on their own lives and bodies.

Landscape painter Victoria Adams arrives in late March from Vashon Island in the Puget Sound. Inspired by the weather, sky and land of the Pacific Northwest, Adams' work combines her memories of paintings and places that suggest timeless views of the landscape.

Derrick Guild, a native of Perth, Scotland, who currently resides on the Island of Ascension in the South Atlantic, completes the season. Guild's detailed paintings of items from vegetables to pastries follow in the tradition of the "kitchen still life," a genre practiced by European masters of the 15th to 19th centuries.

See how their art happens. Visit each artist as they work in studio, and take in specially curated exhibits that help to place the creative process in the context of their work.

LUX

#2
December
January
February
2008/2009

A Site to Behold!

FROM THE DIRECTOR

November marks the first anniversary of the Lux facility. It's been a year of constant change as we hosted six resident artists from around the globe, each bringing their unique vision to life.

In addition to the new events and programs we've introduced as part of our residency program, Lux has recently grown in size, too. On October 1, we became owners of the property that fronts El Camino Real at the base of our driveway. The parcel contains a 6,626-square-foot building, and gives Lux strategic street-front visibility, while providing a gateway to our facility and an eventual home for Lux's growing education programs.

This December, to celebrate our success, we invite the public to enjoy a month of free admission. We hope that you will use this opportunity to share the Lux experience with your friends and families. Be our guest this holiday season, and be a part of making art happen!

Reeny Shaw

This fall, Lux proudly expands its collection of on-site art installations with the addition of a monumental sculpture by artist Robert Lobe.

Entitled *Mother Maple*, the piece depicts the lower part of a tree trunk, a branch, and a large rock, and is made of heat-treated, hammered aluminum. Created by Lobe in 1988, it measures an impressive 120" high by 125" wide by 108" deep and weighs 300 pounds.

To create his sculptures, Lobe uses an adaptation of repoussé, a technique in which metal is hammered, usually from the inside, to create a specific design or form.

Commonly used by ancient Greeks in the fabrication of armor, its most iconic example is likely the Statue of Liberty.

Lobe encases trees and rocks in sheets of aluminum, using mallets and a pneumatic air compressor to stretch and tighten the metal. Through the force of repetitive blows from the mallets and hammers, Lobe alters the structure of the aluminum until it stretches and conforms snugly to the texture of the rock or tree, replicating and abstracting the contours, then enhancing the play of light and shadow on the surfaces.

Lobe, who had visited Lux in the spring, saw the potential in its native-landscaped environment serving as a fitting site for *Mother Maple*. In addition to complementing *Bucket with Abstraction*, a smaller sculpture by Lobe in the Lux library, *Mother Maple* joins several installations that have been incorporated into the Lux landscape. These include two by former artists-in-residence, *Tower* by Daniel Wheeler and *Garden of Apple Delights* by Astrid Preston, as well as *Home* by Ali Acerol.

Mother Maple was recently moved to Lux from its previous public installation in Palm Desert. It stands near the top of Lux's granite trail and is on loan to the Institute through October 2010.

ABOUT ROBERT LOBE

Since beginning his career in the late 1960s, environmental artist Robert Lobe has become best known for his aluminum cast sculptures and reliefs that simultaneously pay homage to nature and serve as a cautionary message of human alienation from the natural.

His creations have been commissioned and exhibited in galleries and museums nationwide, including the Solomon R. Guggenheim Museum, the Whitney Museum of American Art, the National Gallery, and the Museum of Contemporary Art in Los Angeles.

Lux thanks the following donors for their invaluable support in the purchase of the new acreage and education center at 1576 El Camino Real.

Joyce & Stanley Black
Linda Brandes
Diane & Christopher Calkins
Linda & Wally Dieckmann

Karen & Craig Edwards
Lynn & Jim Finkelstein
Jennifer & Barry Greenberg
Ann Hunter-Welborn & David Welborn

Carl & Malene Kokkonen
La Jolla Bank
Gayle Mellison
Lauren & Rainer Mengling

Reeny & David Shaw
Trudy Stambrook & Paul Robinson
Supervisor Pam Slater-Price & the County of San Diego

Karen & Stuart Tanz
Linda & Ron Tenko
Jean Walcher
Jeanine & Frank Warren

Cover: Jolynn Krystosek, Verdure Series, Outfield 3 (detail), 2007. Wax, 19x16"x9x46".

LUX

#3
March
April
May
2009

Luxurious Design

FROM THE DIRECTOR

As Lux celebrates our second full season, we continue to redefine the museum experience. Starting this spring, Lux begins our Studio Series, inviting a noted artist, historian, or critic to discuss the work on the Lux studio walls. Enlightening and inviting, it offers a chance to ask questions, share our views, and hear the artists' responses to the artists' visions.

No matter which artist is on exhibit, there is magic in the air of the Lux studio. It's not just the art, but the way everything comes together: the award-winning architecture, the captivating view of the native landscape, and the artists drawing, painting, cutting, and shaping a unique work inspired by what they find here.

Form meets materials are transformed. The excitement builds as images grow, colors change, and new forms emerge. Visit Lux and experience the magic.

Reeny Shaw

"luxuriously executed from top to bottom"
— THE SAN DIEGO ARCHITECTURAL FOUNDATION

Since inaugurating our permanent facility just over a year ago, Lux has become known as the place to see works of art created before your eyes. Now Lux has been recognized as a work of art itself.

This fall, the San Diego Architectural Foundation awarded the 2008 Grand Orchid—its highest honor—to the Lux Artist Pavilion, citing the many unique design and eco-friendly features the jury called "luxuriously executed from top to bottom."

Lux was chosen from among 258 nominees and topped the list of 20 Orchids awarded as part of the foundation's Orchids & Onions ceremony, which recognizes the best and worst in San Diego architecture, landscaping and sustainable design. Projects are nominated by the public and selected by an eight-member jury comprised of regional architects and design professionals.

Designed by Santa Monica-based architect Renzo Zecchetto, Lux was one of the first cultural facilities in the region built with an eye toward environmental sustainability. Zecchetto—whose other works include the recently unveiled and critically acclaimed Eli and Edith Broad Stage at Santa Monica City College—incorporated several energy-saving strategies and original design features.

Visitors to the facility are familiar with the unique sliding wall that opens to the native landscape and lulls beyond, as well as the light dropping in from the four angled light monitors that tower like guardians 20 feet above. Unseen are features such as the Pavilion's use of recycled building materials that will help save resources for future generations.

Slated to be the first LEED-certified "green" art museum in California, the Artist Pavilion is only the first phase of the envisioned Lux site. With the addition of a planned second pavilion, the completed Lux campus will serve as a model for sustainable design and construction across the region—and the place to see art happen in one of San Diego's most artful environments.

Osim u kuhinji, maslinovo ulje
koristimo u domaćinstvu,
medicini, kozmetici,
aromaterapiji i dr.
Zato ostanete li bez skupih
kozmetičkih preparata,
ne očajavajte, maslinovo ulje
će ih dostojno zamijeniti.
Primjerice, njime na komadiću
vate možete jednostavno
odstraniti make-up, pa i onaj
tvrdokornije vrste, primjerice

vodootpornu maskaru.
Nije tajna da je maslinovo ulje
sastavni dio brojnih krema,
njime se omekšava koža,
rade maske za njegu kože
ruku, noktiju i stopala, stavlja
kao regenerator na kosu.
Njegova primjena se
preporučuje i kod njege suhe
i nadražene kože, a pomaže
i pri zacijeljivanju rana
i ogrebotina.

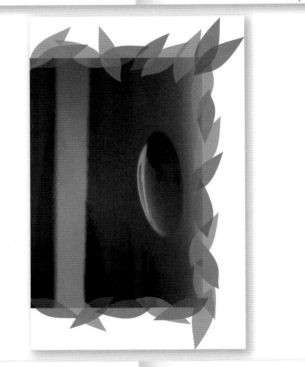

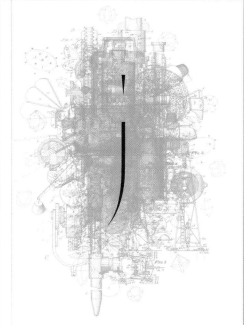

Mytton Williams
Topless Calendar
2010

July

M	T	W	T	F	S	S	M	T	W	T	F	S	S
28	29	30	01	02	03	04	05	06	07	08	09	10	11
12	13	14	15	16	17	18	19	20	21	22	23	24	25
26	27	28	29	30	31	01	02	03	04	05	06	07	08

11 / World Cup Final
myttonwilliams.co.uk

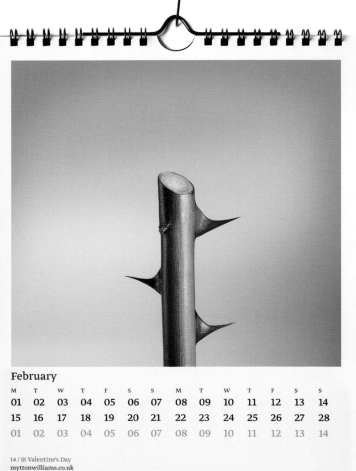

February

M	T	W	T	F	S	S	M	T	W	T	F	S	S
01	02	03	04	05	06	07	08	09	10	11	12	13	14
15	16	17	18	19	20	21	22	23	24	25	26	27	28
01	02	03	04	05	06	07	08	09	10	11	12	13	14

14 / St Valentine's Day
myttonwilliams.co.uk

June

M	T	W	T	F	S	S	M	T	W	T	F	S	S
31	01	02	03	04	05	06	07	08	09	10	11	12	13
14	15	16	17	18	19	20	21	22	23	24	25	26	27
28	29	30	01	02	03	04	05	06	07	08	09	10	11

20 / Father's Day
myttonwilliams.co.uk

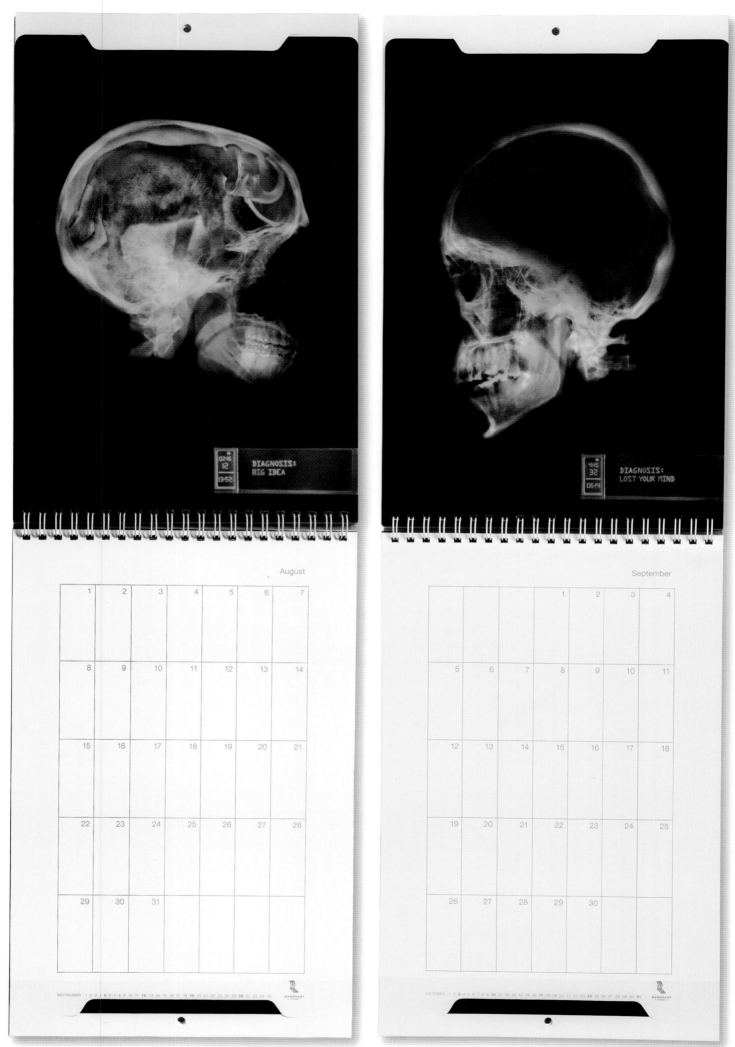

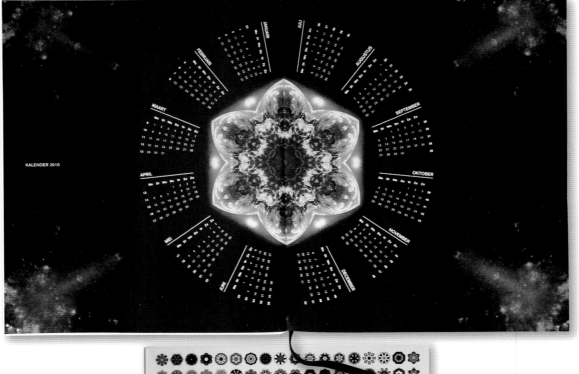

JAN

					1	2
3	4	5	6	7	8	9
10	11	12	13	14	15	16
17	18	19	20	21	22	23
24	25	26	27	28	29	30
31						

lee hanson copywriter

A self-proclaimed freak dancer with a hankering for all things huge (he's seen 41 of the World's Largest Things), Lee has a lot to bring to the dance floor. "The Sprinkler" aside, helping charity is certainly one of his best moves.

FEB

	1	2	3	4	5	6
7	8	9	10	11	12	13
14	15	16	17	18	19	20
21	22	23	24	25	26	27
28						

joe monnens senior designer

A modern-day Paul Bunyan, this rugged beefcake likes to swing his axe around. But while giant, Joe's charitable deeds transcend ordinary folklore.

JULY

			1	2	3	
4	5	6	7	8	9	10
11	12	13	14	15	16	17
18	19	20	21	22	23	24
25	26	27	28	29	30	31

micah dahl assistant editor

Despite a strong backhand—and an even stronger backside—Micah cares less about acing his opponent than he does about giving others the advantage. So, whether that means sprouting a mustache or sporting hot pants, he's always up for the challenge.

AUG

1	2	3	4	5	6	7
8	9	10	11	12	13	14
15	16	17	18	19	20	21
22	23	24	25	26	27	28
29	30	31				

john frahm, dan mandle, mike schwab & aaron o'keefe account management

Whoever said tandem bikes weren't sexy, never met these guys. What's hotter? Four guys working in tandem to do something remarkable for the greater good.

Wait — only two more.

NOV

	1	2	3	4	5	6
7	8	9	10	11	12	13
14	15	16	17	18	19	20
21	22	23	24	25	26	27
28	29	30				

braden stadlman
senior interactive producer

It's possible that every man has an inner bad boy. Ironically, Braden's rocker alter ego has only managed to help him do good things for others. Rock on.

DEC

		1	2	3	4	
5	6	7	8	9	10	11
12	13	14	15	16	17	18
19	20	21	22	23	24	25
26	27	28	29	30	31	

sawyer blur senior contact planner

Inspired by a love of Harry Potter, and the only guy who can make knee-high striped socks look sexy, Sawyer is proud to finally perform some of his own magic: giving back to ordinary folks, or *muggles*, as Harry (and Sawyer) might say.

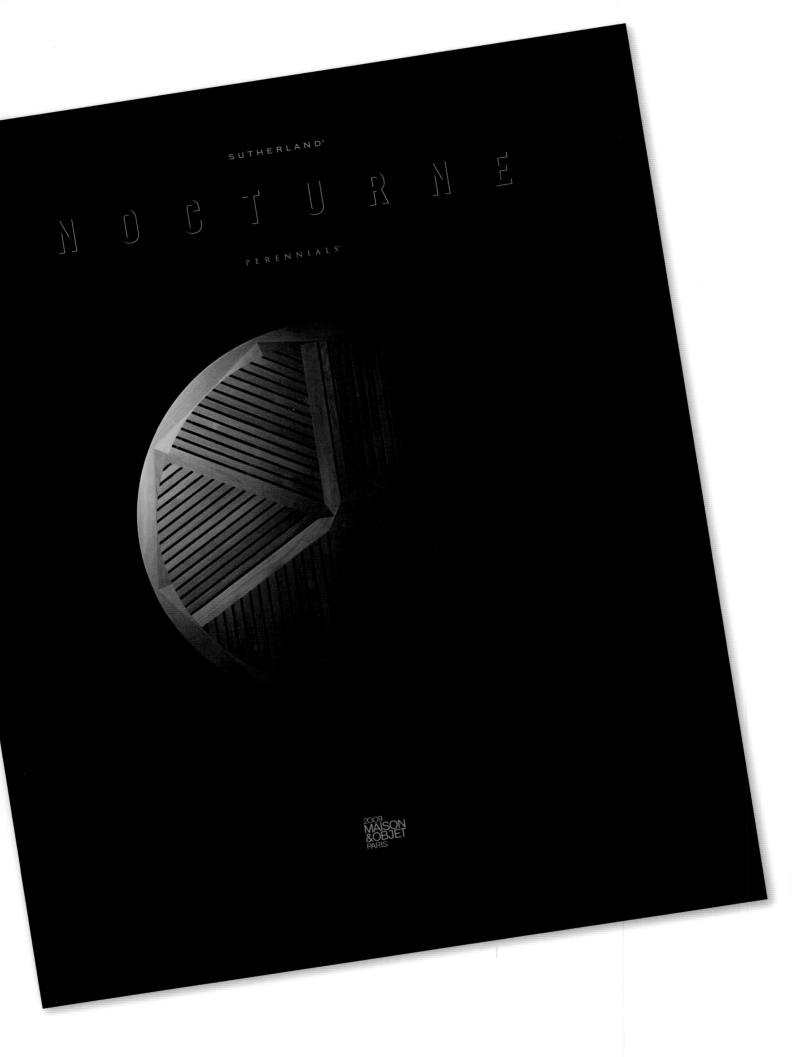

SUTHERLAND

PERENNIALS

NOCTURNE

2009
MAISON
&OBJET
PARIS

Design Within Reach
Organization for Every Room
February 2009

What do designers do when chaos overtakes order? They build something that solves the problem. Our new **Cubitec Shelving** (p.4) is one

such example, newly designed in two depths to better suit a variety of uses in any room, office or retail space. If "out of sight, out of mind" is more your mantra, consider a **Nexus Storage Cube** (dwr.com) with a big interior and a top that works as a tray. As for what to serve on that tray, whip up a dish with the space-planned **Kitchen Organizer** (p.8) that keeps even the most unruly of chefs in order. To keep your dining area organized, use the cart for serving and clearing. If your workspace needs organizing, may we suggest one of our **Workspace Packages** (p.10-11). Each one includes a desk, chair and lamp. You can even find the actual space to work in with our prefab **Kithaus** (p.23). For more sleep and storage, the **Matera Bed** satisfies both needs, and it's part of our Bedroom and Mattress Sale (p.20-22), now through Tuesday, February 10.

DESIGN
WITHIN
REACH

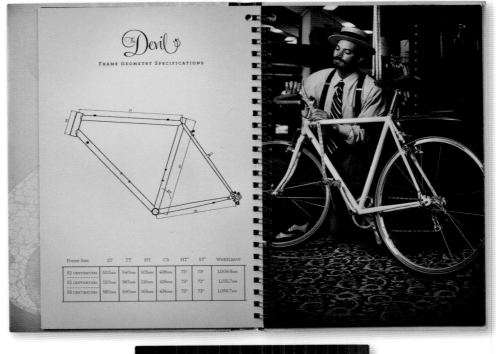

The Devil

FRAME GEOMETRY SPECIFICATIONS

Frame Size	ST	TT	HT	CS	HT°	ST°	WHEELBASE
52 CENTIMETERS	520mm	540mm	105mm	436mm	73°	73°	1,006.8mm
55 CENTIMETERS	550mm	565mm	135mm	436mm	73°	73°	1,031.7mm
58 CENTIMETERS	580mm	590mm	165mm	436mm	73°	73°	1,056.7mm

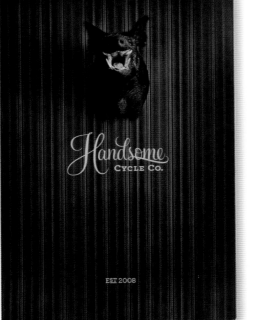

Handsome CYCLE CO.

EST 2008

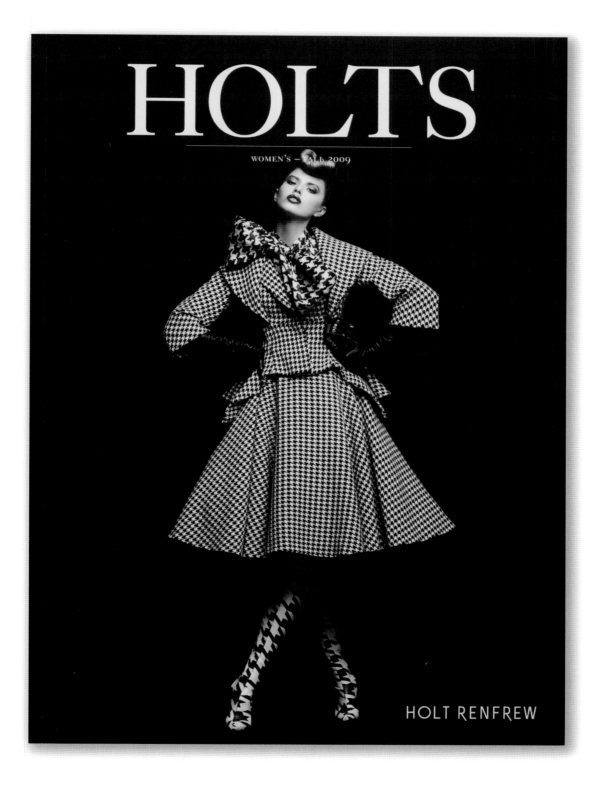

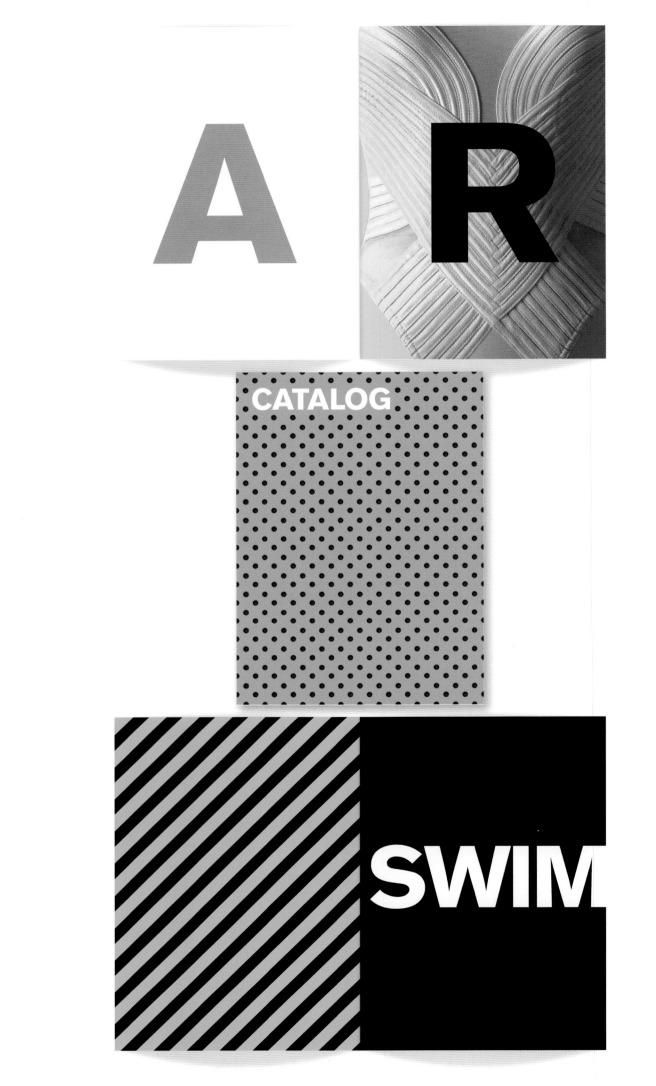

A R

CATALOG

SWIM

The 2010 CVO™ Fat Bob™ model is all about cutting edge style. With exclusive Midnight Pearl™ chrome components, three unique paint sets and a distressed brown leather seat, this machine not only exudes style but has 110 cubic inches of killer performance.

CVO™ FXDFSE2 FAT BOB™

HARLEY-DAVIDSON®
2010 CUSTOM VEHICLE OPERATIONS™ MOTORCYCLES

CVO® SOFTAIL® CONVERTIBLE

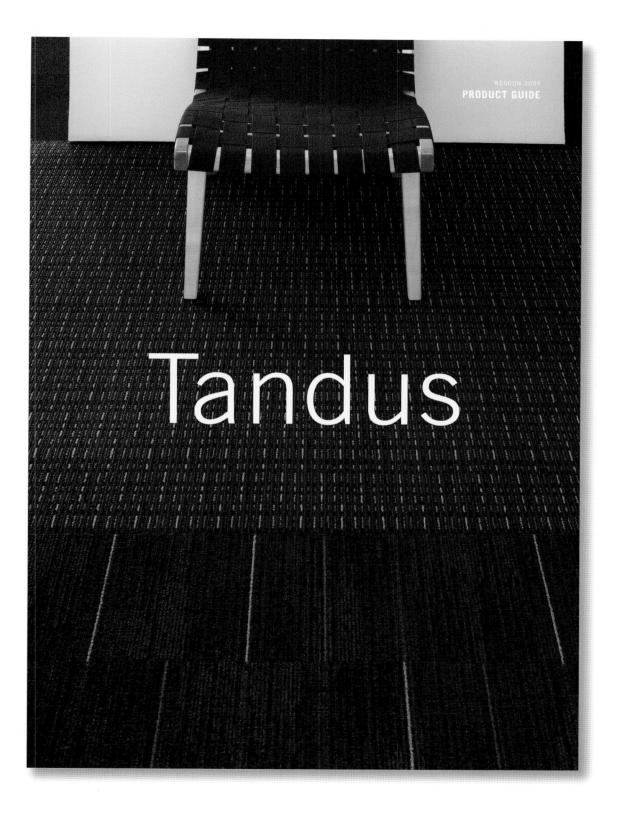

NEOCON 2009
PRODUCT GUIDE

Tandus

Setu is simple.
Setu is motion.
Setu is adaptable.

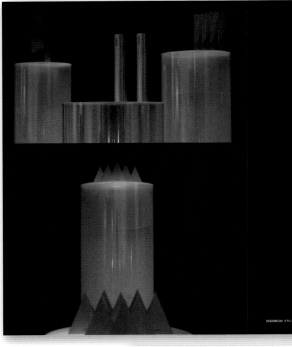

Ishinho

Ishinho is a book of medicine compiled over a thousand years ago by the medical expert, Tanba no Yasunori. In 984, Tanba presented his encyclopedic work, the oldest of its kind in Japan, to Emperor En'yuu. It was one of 200 works on medicine, immortality, Buddhism, philosophy and literature written at the time of the Chinese Song Dynasty. *Ishinho* itself was made up of 30 scrolls. It lists more than 1000 animals, plants, minerals and other substances, and presents medical formulas equal to or superior to those used in herbal medicine to cure illness and injury today. For hundreds of years, *Ishinho* was considered a fantasy, as no one had ever seen the entire work, but in the Edo era, the government published a replica printing. Today, *Ishinho* is a National Treasure, stored in the Ninnaji Temple in Kyoto and the Tokyo National Museum. It is considered an important world cultural asset. *Ishinho* is a comprehensive collection of ideas, wisdom and formulas, all aiming to provide the results that humankind will always desire. When we look at *Ishinho* from the viewpoint of modern thought and the latest in technology, we will be even further illuminated.

デザイン力が創り出すブランド

The Brand Created by Design

issimbow

総合ディレクション：松永 真
編集：宣伝会議　編集協力：日本香堂、張心方

茂木 健一郎
脳科学者／ソニーコンピュータサイエンス研究所 シニアリサーチャー

ブランドの根底にある
「奥深い理念」を、
瞬時に認知させる「デザイン力」で
強力に推し進める方法に感動した。

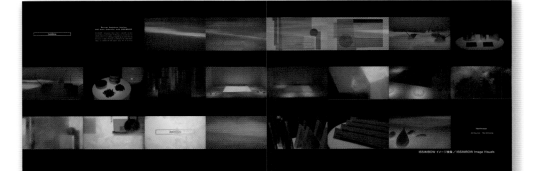

ISSIMBOW イメージ映像

ISSIMBOWは、まずグラフィックデザインがブランドを創った。次にそのコンセプトとデザインに触発され音楽家が音楽を創った。ふたつが融合して映像が創られた。静のグラフィックデザインに動の加わり映像型動が動き出した。その動きは映像作家によってCGアニメーション化されたのみできない。人間の予測できない不可思議なものが加えられた。それは煙である。このスモークは、デコレーション・香司のクリエイターによって、偶然が創り出す美への挑戦となった。グラフィックデザインのときに、現象でとらえられる「気」が自身の身体のように動いていく。偶然性が創り出す生命のように、生命の躍動の姿を思わせる。ブランド発表の会場で展示され映られる影を考えた。この会場のすべての映画監督によって記録され、ひとつの映像作品となった。そして、それらは、ISSIMBOWブランドのアートであるとともに、やがて販売される心身健美の製品郡の前に創られたプロジェクトでもある。

Visuals of ISSIMBOW Brand Images

First of all, graphic design made ISSIMBOW into a brand. Incited by the concept and design, a musician created music. The combination of the two resulted in images. Movement was added to static graphic design to make the visual space move. Not only did a visual creator make CG animation out of that movement, but something else was added—something humans could not predict. Smoke. A decoration formation creator was challenged by the smoke to make a thing of beauty that came from something born incidentally. The graphic design gave qi, an incorporeal visually, movement. It was like a life form. Beauty born of incidence is close to chaos, and reminds us of the source of life. It was aired at the exhibit launching the brand, and was received with enthusiasm. All of this was recorded by a film director and made into a single film. Along with the ISSIMBOW brand art, it will ultimately become a product, one of the line-up of products for beauty and health of heart and mind.

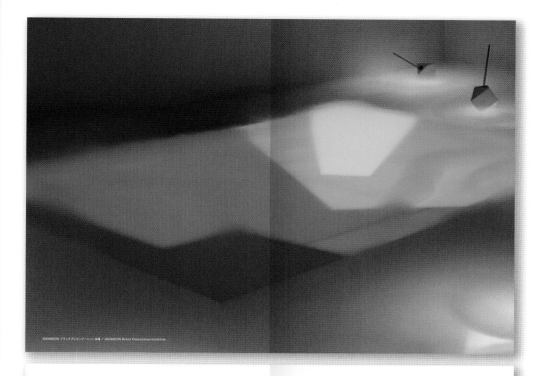

ISSIMBOW ブランドプレゼンテーション 会場／ISSIMBOW Brand Presentation Exhibition

ISSIMBOW Katachi-koh 材料
ISSIMBOW Katachi-koh Materials

Katachi-kohの原料は全22種、古来よりの伝統的香料、現代的原料、世界民間伝承医療原料の中から、［健］［涼］［活］のテーマごとに選び抜かれた素材が用いられている。

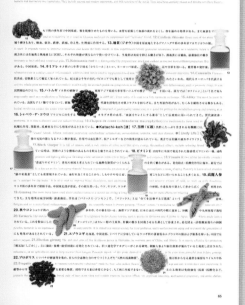

ISSIMBOW ブランドプレゼンテーション 会場／ISSIMBOW Brand Presentation Exhibition

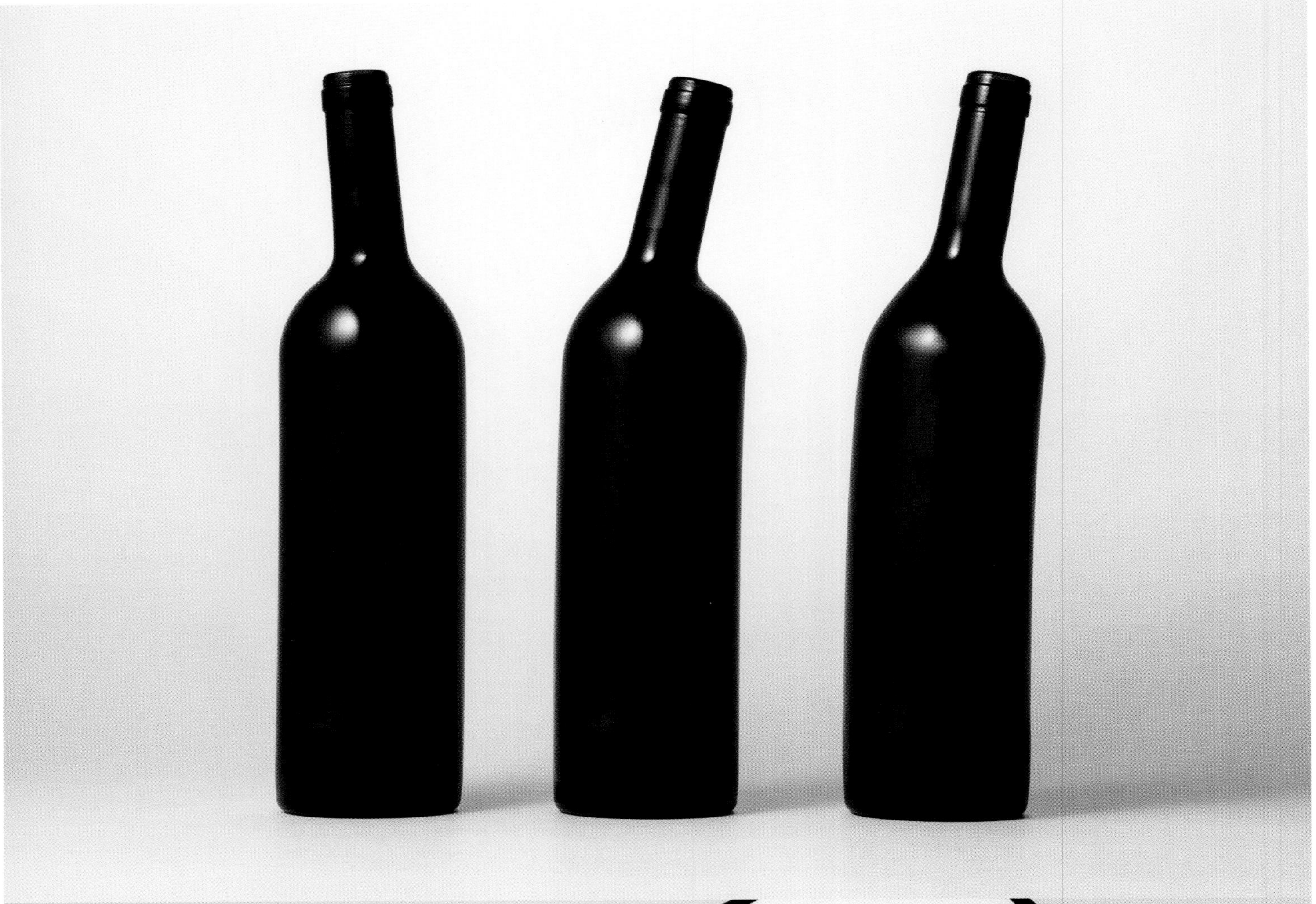

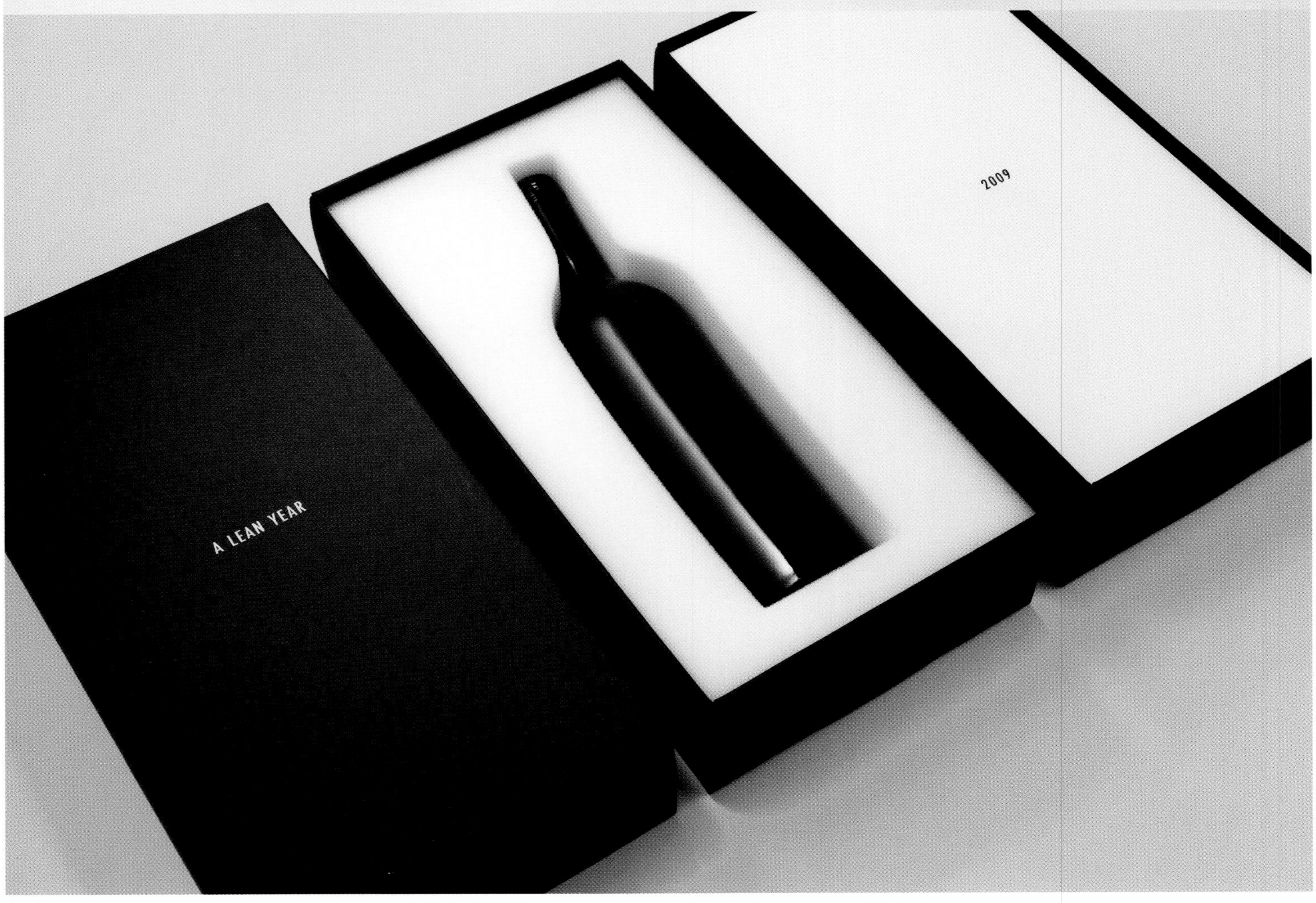

PLATINUM

00:00

HOME	VISITOR
21	02

PERIOD

● ● ● ●

SIX PALE, EARTHBOUND DESK JOCKEYS FROM GQ CHALLENGED THE GREATEST BASKETBALL PLAYER ON EARTH, ALSO KNOWN AS **LeBRON JAMES,** *TO A GAME OF BASKETBALL AT THE TIME AND PLACE OF HIS CHOOSING.*

UNFORTUNATELY, THE CHALLENGE WAS ACCEPTED

BY
JOEL LOVELL

PHOTOGRAPHS BY
NATHANIEL GOLDBERG

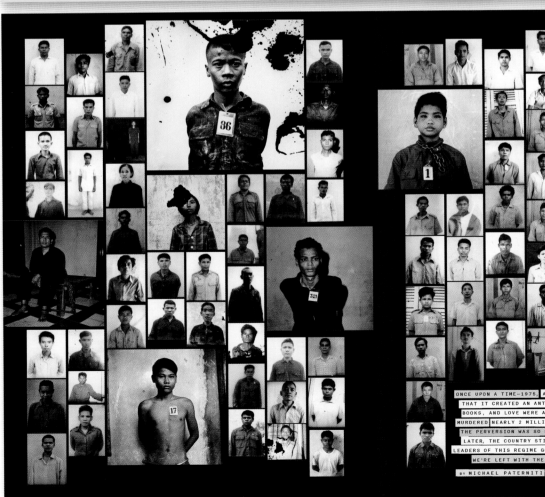

NEVER FORGET

ONCE UPON A TIME—1975, ACTUALLY, IN CAMBODIA—THERE WAS A REGIME SO EVIL THAT IT CREATED AN ANTISOCIETY WHERE TORTURE WAS CURRENCY AND MUSIC, BOOKS, AND LOVE WERE ABOLISHED. THIS REGIME RULED FOR FOUR YEARS AND MURDERED NEARLY 2 MILLION OF ITS CITIZENS, A QUARTER OF THE POPULATION. THE PERVERSION WAS SO EXTREME, THE ACTS SO SAVAGE, THAT THREE DECADES LATER, THE COUNTRY STILL FINDS ITSELF REELING. NOW, AS THE SURVIVING LEADERS OF THIS REGIME GO TO TRIAL AND THE UNIMAGINABLE PAST RISES AGAIN, WE'RE LEFT WITH THE QUESTION: WHAT TOOK US SO LONG TO REMEMBER?
BY MICHAEL PATERNITI

With hundreds of independent music stores going out of business every year, our resident rock correspondent spent two weeks working behind the counter of one of the last stores left standing—and found a place where metal still rules, vinyl still sells, and the 16-year-old clerk ringing you up has never heard of Hannah Montana

**THE LAST
RECORD STORE**

Written by DAN KENNEDY

**A NICE
QUIET CHAT WITH
CHRISTIAN
BALE**

In which the most ardent actor of his generation
speaks of starving for his art, falling asleep
during scenes, and why John Connor —
not CHRISTIAN BALE — bears the lion's share of
the blame for that infamous explosion on the set
of 'Terminator Salvation'

(The G Q & A by ANDREW CORSELLO
Photographs by TERRY RICHARDSON)

120

GQ

TRIUMPH OF HIS WILL

ONLY **QUENTIN TARANTINO** COULD CREATE 'INGLOURIOUS BASTERDS,' WHEREIN **BRAD PITT** PLAYS A REDNECK LEADING A BAND OF TOUGH JEWS BENT ON GOING, WELL, MEDIEVAL ON NAZIS. AND THAT'S JUST ONE PART OF HIS NEW MOVIE. **ALEX PAPPADEMAS** FOLLOWS THE MOST AMBITIOUS DIRECTOR OF HIS GENERATION FROM BERLIN TO CANNES TO LOS ANGELES AS HE STRUGGLES TO FINISH WHAT HE HOPES WILL BE HIS NEW MASTERPIECE // PHOTOGRAPHS BY **MARK SELIGER**.GQ.AUG.87

← TARANTINO IN HIS OFFICE OVERLOOKING THE SAN FERNANDO VALLEY. THE AWARDS COLLECTION INCLUDES THE OSCAR AND PALME D'OR FOR 'PULP FICTION' AND HIS AMERICAN CHOREOGRAPHY AWARD FOR 'KILL BILL.'

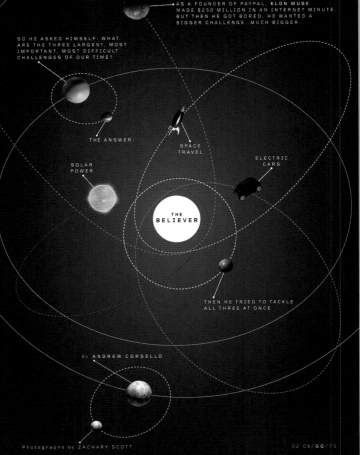

AS A FOUNDER OF PAYPAL, ELON MUSK MADE $250 MILLION IN AN INTERNET MINUTE. BUT THEN HE GOT BORED. HE WANTED A BIGGER CHALLENGE. MUCH BIGGER.

SO HE ASKED HIMSELF: WHAT ARE THE THREE LARGEST, MOST IMPORTANT, MOST DIFFICULT CHALLENGES OF OUR TIME?

THE ANSWER:

SPACE TRAVEL

SOLAR POWER

ELECTRIC CARS

THE BELIEVER

THEN HE TRIED TO TACKLE ALL THREE AT ONCE

By ANDREW CORSELLO

Photographs by ZACHARY SCOTT

02 09/**GQ**/75

MIX:
one part Greek hillbilly
with one part
absurdist humor

ADD:
Sarah Silverman,
gigantic beard,
intense fear of fame

WAIT:
fifteen years,
then finish off with
dollop of
instant superstardom

THE
PERFECTLY AGED
WEIRDNESS
OF
ZACH
GALIFIANAKIS

READ HERE

177

PHOTOGRAPHS BY
MARTIN SCHOELLER

BY
DEVIN
FRIEDMAN
100% GQ

GENTLEMEN'S QUARTERLY

Oh, Betty!

JANUARY JONES spent years in Hollywood smiling through role after role as Babe #4 before landing a part as **BETTY DRAPER** on 'Mad Men'—the most complex, mysterious woman on television today. And if you want to understand where America's sexiest housewife comes from? Just ask January—over a few too many beers—how she got to where she is today

by **MARK KIRBY**
Photographs by **TERRY RICHARDSON**

NOV/158

noi.se

number 24

BEAUTY DESIGN FASHION CULTURE

METAL

DYLAN MARTOREL, MIGUEL ... LOBOS, KRIS VAN ASSCHE,
JEREMY JAY, NICO, JAVIER MON... JEREMY SCOTT, XEVI MUNTANÉ,
CARIN WESTER, DIRK MERTEN, AGGTELEK, CHRISTOPHE KUTNER, STEFAN MILEV,
RUMI NEELY, RYŌ KŌBŌ

#16 / JUNIO-JULIO(AGOSTO) 2009
Spain 5€ / Austria, France, Germany 18€
Belgium, Greece, Italy, Portu... UK 9€

MUSE

The Fashionart Magazine

NATASHA OBSESSED

BILINGUAL WITH
ENGLISH TEXT

SUPER TROUPER

PHOTOGRAPHY
SØLVE SUNDSBØ

t-shirt vintage *Chanel*,
necklaces and bracelets
Burberry Prorsum;
trousers *Rue Du Mail by Martine*
Sitbon; trousers hanging
necklace *Erickson Beamon*;
studded jacket and denim shorts
Boss; gloves *LaCrasia*;
necklace worn around
left and right leg *Burberry*
Prorsum; boxing mouth
guard *Doc Ultimate*
Sports & Apparel

FASHION MARIE CHAIX

122

WARM
L EATH ERETTE

PHOTOGRAPHY
DAVID SHERRY

FASHION KATIE ...

HOG

FOR THE HARLEY-DAVIDSON® *ENTHUSIAST* SINCE 1916

$4.99US

001

THE XR1200™ COMES HOME   THRASHING THE IRON 883™   BUENOS AIRES AT REST

HOG

FOR THE HARLEY-DAVIDSON® *ENTHUSIAST* SINCE 1916

004

CUSTOM VEHICLE OBSERVATIONS

HOG

FOR THE HARLEY-DAVIDSON® *ENTHUSIAST* SINCE 1916

$4.99US

003

FULL THROTTLE FOR 2010   50 STATES IN 50 DAYS   DIGGING DEEP AT THE MILE

HOG

FOR THE HARLEY-DAVIDSON® *ENTHUSIAST* SINCE 1916

002

REINTRODUCING THE FL   AROUND THE WORLD IN 4,636 DAYS   READERS REACT

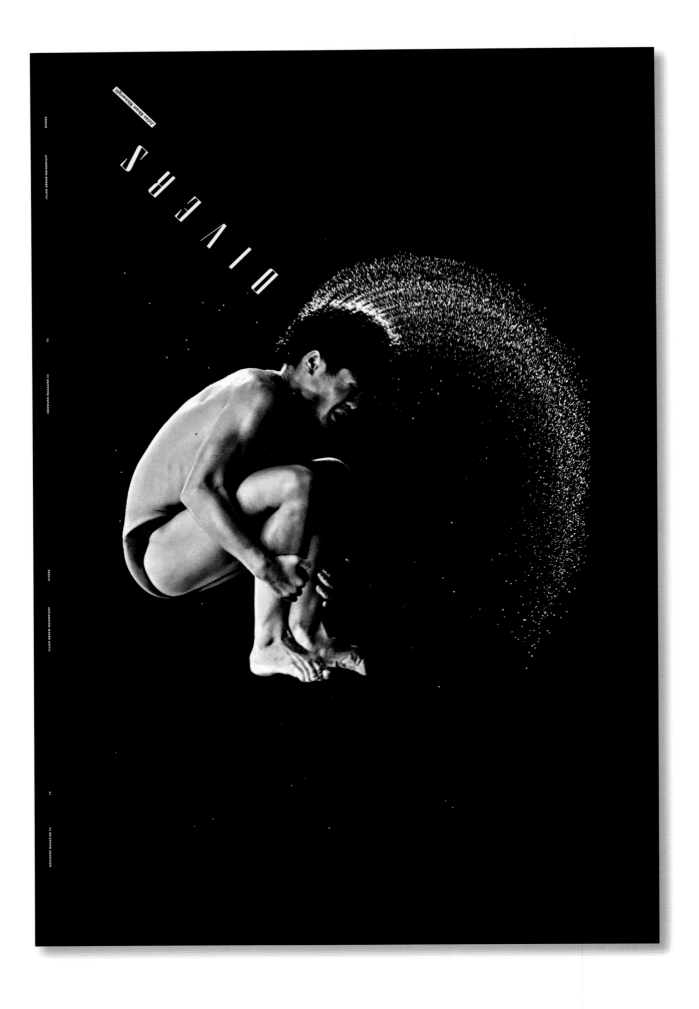

DIVERS

JULIAN ABRAM WAINWRIGHT

NEWYORK MAGAZINE 04

Johnston Works www.johnstonworks.com (top) | **Brunswick Group LLP**
Visual Arts Press, Ltd. www.sva.edu/publishing/index.jsp?sid0=81&sid1=82 (middle) | **School of Visual Arts**
Underline Studio www.underlinestudio.com (bottom) | **Prefix Institute of Contemporary Arts** | **Editorial 109**

LUSH

FASHION + ART

WONDER-
LAND

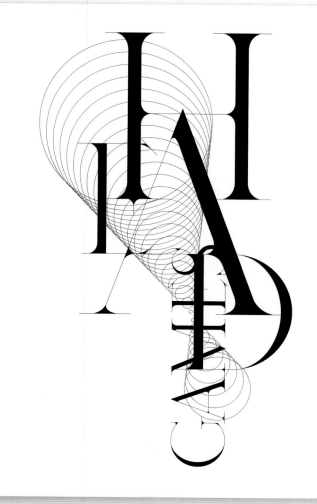

HEAD GAMES

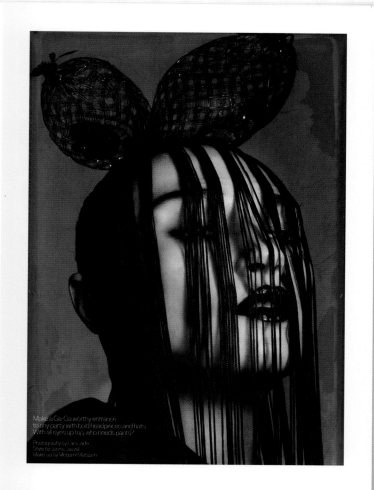

Make a Ga-Ga worthy entrance
to any party with bold headpieces and hats.
With all eyes up top, who needs pants?

Photography by Lara Jade
Style by Janine Jarrell
Make-up by Megumi Matsunn

UP TOWN GIRL

This winter, explore tonal dressing in browns, from cream and
caramel to chocolate and sepia. Coupling softness and strength,
you can be the lady without giving up the girl.

Photography by Christopher Micaud
Style by Pascale Grisé

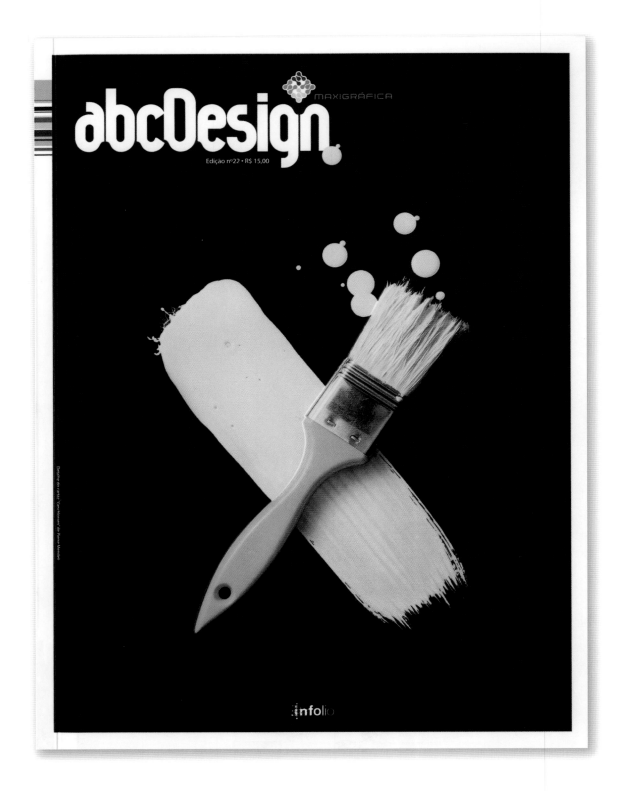

design mind

In the hours before his sub-freezing swim (water temperature: 29°F or -1.7°C) across the North Pole in 2007, TEDGlobal speaker Lewis Pugh prepared like any other athlete — he listened to his iPod.

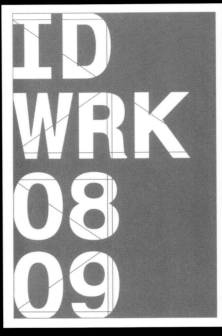

ID
WRK
08
09

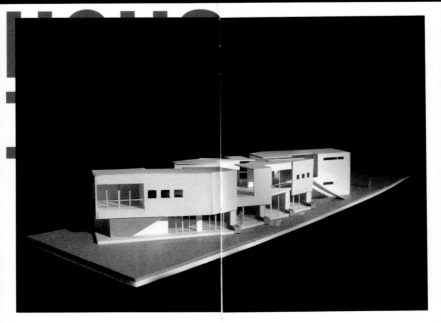

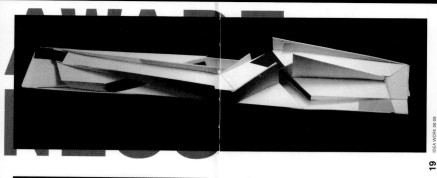

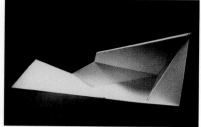

ARCH 102A
AWARENESS

COORDINATOR: Lee Olvera. INSTRUCTORS: Valery Augustin,
Mira Drew, Michael Chung, Rebecca Lowry, Lauren Matchison,
Janice Shimizu, Linda Taalman and Rennie Tang.

The first year design studio is the introduction to architecture as cultural practice based on ideas. The production
of outstanding work is dependent on both design intent
and technical skills, developed through diligent and con-
tinuous practice. The ability to embody design work with
meaningful intentions only arises through investigation
and research, resulting in a collected body of knowledge
used in the production of one's own work. The application
of this scholarship in design is directed by critical thinking,
utilizing insight and discerning intellect in the creative application of knowledge.

The semester began with composition-based projects
designed to heighten skills of observation, perception,
analysis and transformation by employing oppositional
relationships: realism and abstraction, line and surface,
object and space, 2-D shape and 3-D form. Students uti-
lized multiple means of reiterative exploration to complete
their work, including documentary photography, photo-
collage, drawing and paper-model making, to provoke
inquiry and hone an understanding and appreciation of

design awareness, intent, and meaning—the foundation
of the semester.

The subsequent series of projects explored concepts of
architectural space: scale, movement, transition, materi-
ality, light and context. Building upon the understanding
gained in previous projects, students were given hypo-
thetical, though specific programs and sites. Confronting
the spatial and formal consequences of program and site
through the means of physical and material constraints,
the projects further developed each student's critical inquiry, transcending design principles through architecture.

The culture of the design studio, new to first-year students,
nurtured critical inquiry through disciplined studio work
habits and constructive instructor and peer dialogue. The
process of conceptual exploration, methodology of critical
input, and practice of reiterative refinement were all es-
sential to the informed development of their architecture.

THIS PAGE: (1) OSAMA IGAB, (2) DANIEL KIM
NEXT PAGE: (1) TRISTAN MCGUIRE, (2) HYO NA CHUNG,
(3) SPENCER SANCHEZ, (4) PHUOC NGUYEN

ARCH 505AL
MEDIA, INFILL, AND THE CREATIVE WORKPLACE
INSTRUCTOR: Richard Corsini

This project consisted of a mixed use urban infill building
for a leading creative advertising agency on a corner lot in
downtown Santa Monica. The program posed contradic-
tory modes for the conveyance of meaning: the physicality
of place and material and the ephemerality of image. The
intention was to give the students rich conceptual opportunities for critical discourse regarding language, media
and meaning in contemporary society as well as creative
solutions for an unconventional workplace.

The site conditions and context were straightforward,
and the program was not technically complex so em-
phasis could be placed on a high degree of design and
tectonic resolution. The first half of the semester focused on the overall conceptual and design development of the project. The second half focused on detail
and tectonic development of the design concept and
integration of building systems.

The studio focused on the problem of developing a physical and functional identity expressing the philosophy
and values of an organization and its outward representation and internal operation. Alternative methods of
representation were explored through metaphor, symbol-
ism, and abstract association developed through tectonic

expression and the strategic ordering of form and use.
Alternative organizational strategies were explored to nur-
ture a creative workplace. The objective was to transcend
the use of iconography alone as signifier by the purposeful
organization of function and habitation.

(1) (2) (3) ERIC ANDERSON

OUTER PAGES: Sean Dermond, 4th year; Shooting the film Liberty in Saratoga, NY. Photographs by Sean Dermond and Allison Noel.

191

LEFT PAGE: Jong Do Kim, 4th year
RIGHT PAGE: Han Hu, 4th year

153

LEFT PAGE: Sarah Jane Grosuman, 4th year
RIGHT PAGE: Natalie Krick, 4th year

425

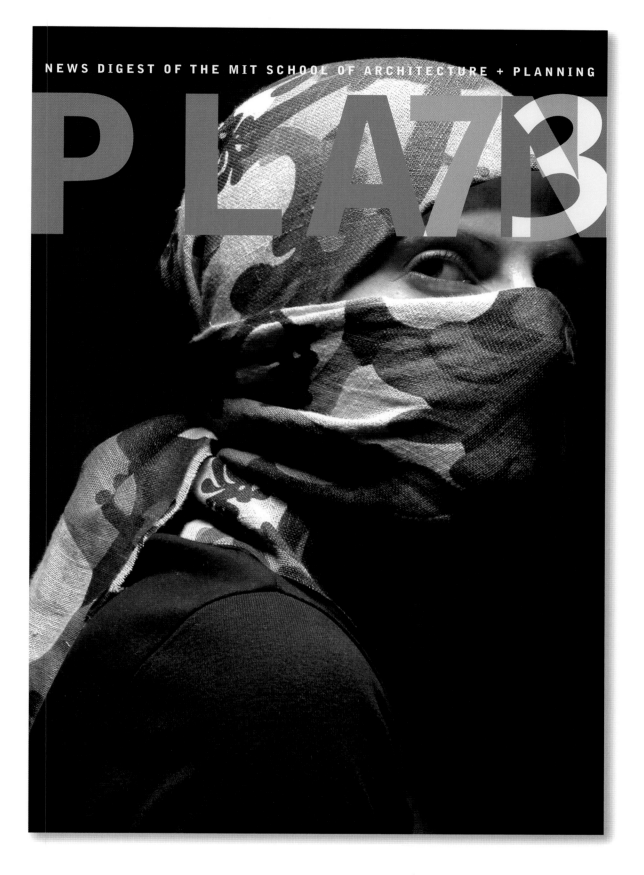

PLA73

601
Artbook
Project
2009

Balance

601
Artbook
Project
2009

Harmony

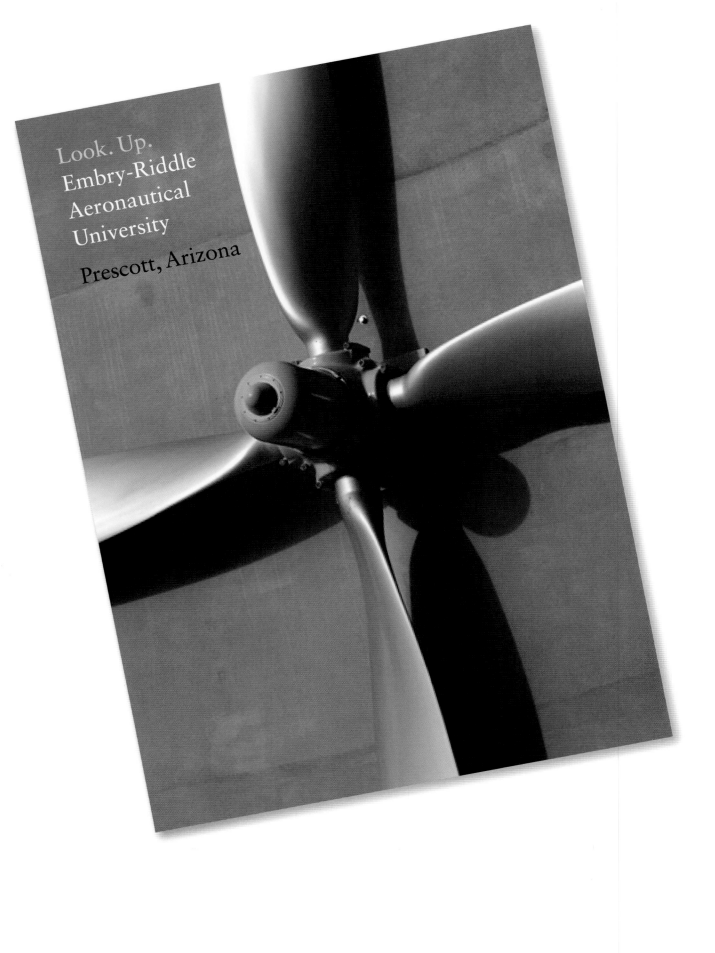

Look. Up.
Embry-Riddle
Aeronautical
University

Prescott, Arizona

Precision, Speed, Experience

"In the last few years, we have invested millions in our facilities, and right now they are as good as they get in this country. Our goal is not just to transfer information but to get students to create new knowledge."

DAN CARRELL
Executive Vice President and Chief Operating Officer,
Embry-Riddle Aeronautical University

"NASA donated our charged coupled device (CCD) debris telescope. It's optimized for tracking rapidly moving near-Earth objects, such as satellites and space debris, as well as asteroids."

DR. BRIAN RACHFORD
Assistant Professor, Physics

"Simulators are more sensitive than airplanes. Master a maneuver in the simulator, and it will be easier in the air."

D.J. CASSADY
Flight Simulator Technician

Take the Controls

You're in Charge

If You Build It …

10 TOP FACILITIES

1. AXFAB

2. Weather Station

3. ADS-B Lab

4. Campus Observatory Complex

5. The Space Systems Lab

6. Robertson Aviation Safety Center I

7. Tracy Doryland Wind Tunnel Laboratory

8. King Engineering and Technology Center

9. The Student Union

10. Silver-Hurz Library and Learning Center

WHERE GREAT PIONEERS MEET

DORNIER
MUSEUM
FRIEDRICHSHAFEN

KNOWLEDGE IS POWER.

ATTITUDE IS EVERYTHING.

Anonymous
Jean M. Scholer
Aragona Family Foundation
Mr. and Mrs. Jim Frazier
Windfall Foundation
Tench and Simone Coxe   Angela and Morton Topfer

Founders Circle

LIVESTRONG

Steve Hicks and Donna Stockton-Hicks
Jennifer Vickers and Lee Walker
Andrew T. Sheehan
The Armstrong Family   James C. Kennedy
Brad A. Silverberg
Carol and Mike Sherwin
Thomas Weisel   Bonita and Jeff Garvey
Kramer Foundation
Craig B. Malloy

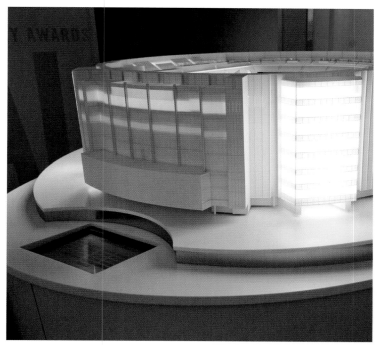

THE STORYTELLER'S ART

A RETROSPECTIVE OF THE WORK OF DESIGNER KIT HINRICHS
FEBRUARY 27 – MAY 3, 2009 | ALYCE DE ROULET WILLIAMSON GALLERY
ART CENTER COLLEGE OF DESIGN | PASADENA, CALIFORNIA

On the wall: WorkplaceOne is a new planning concept that anticipates change and enables workers to adjust their work environments

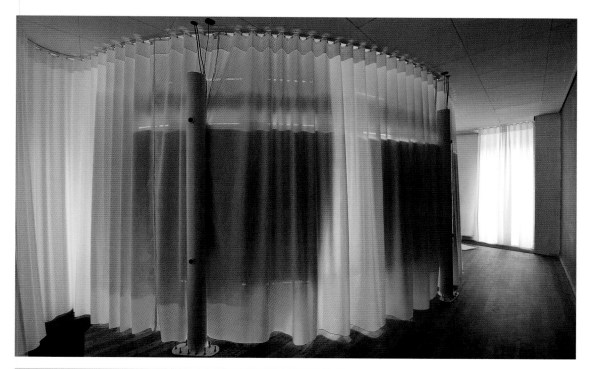

PLATINUM

Robert Rodriguez www.lindgrensmith.com/search/rodriguez/about.php | **United States Postal Service** | Illustration **147**

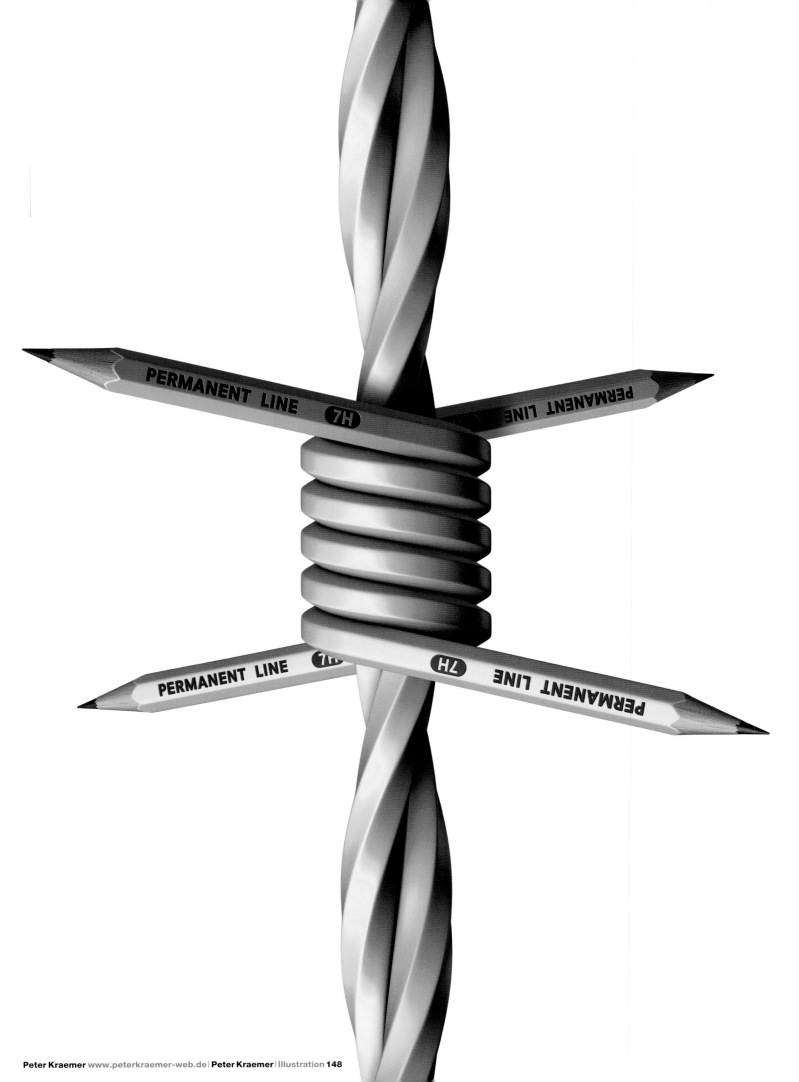

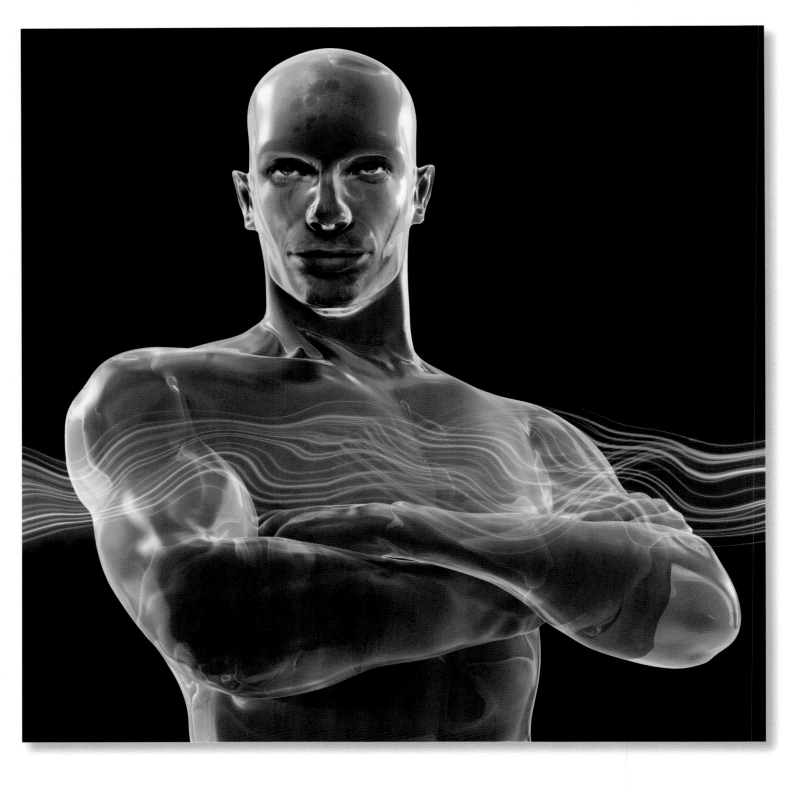

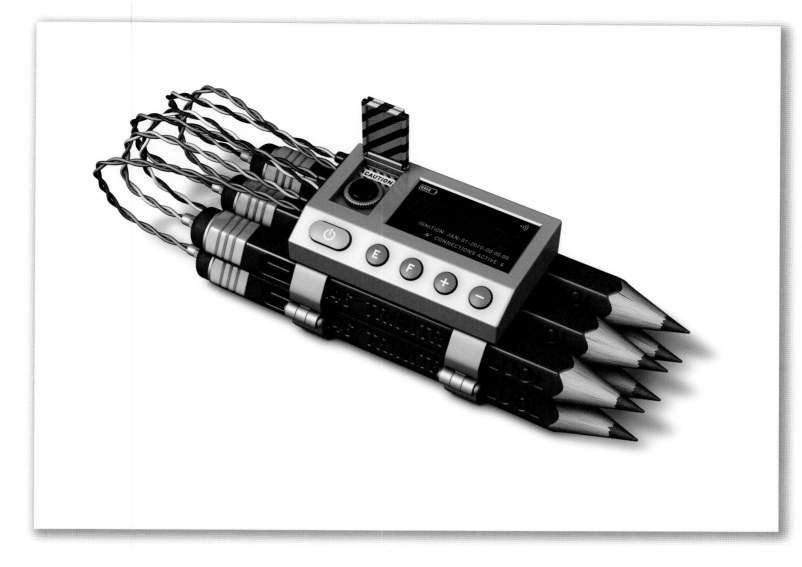

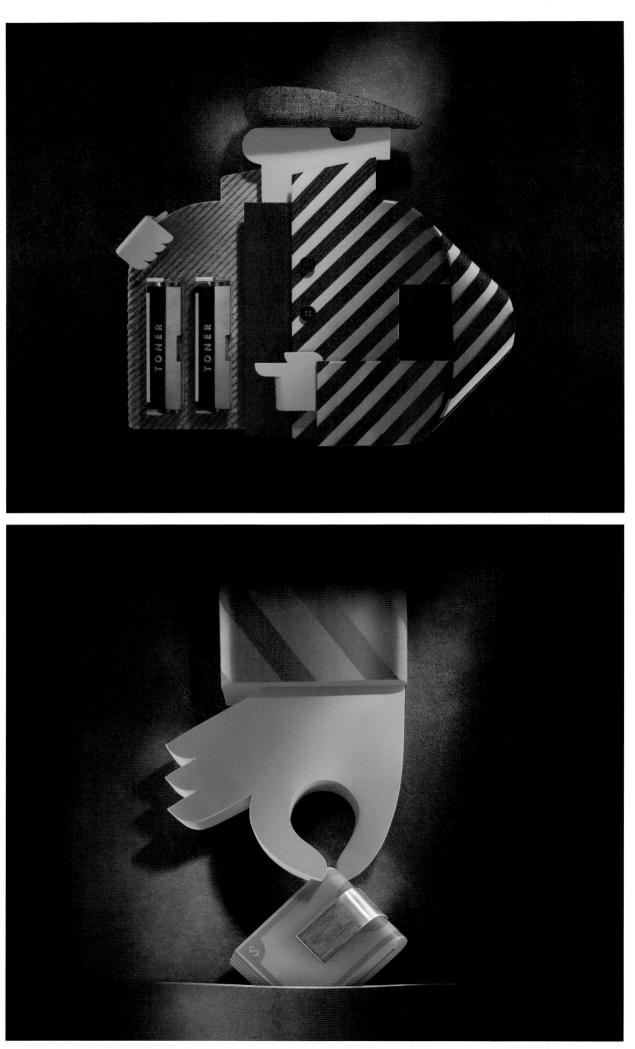

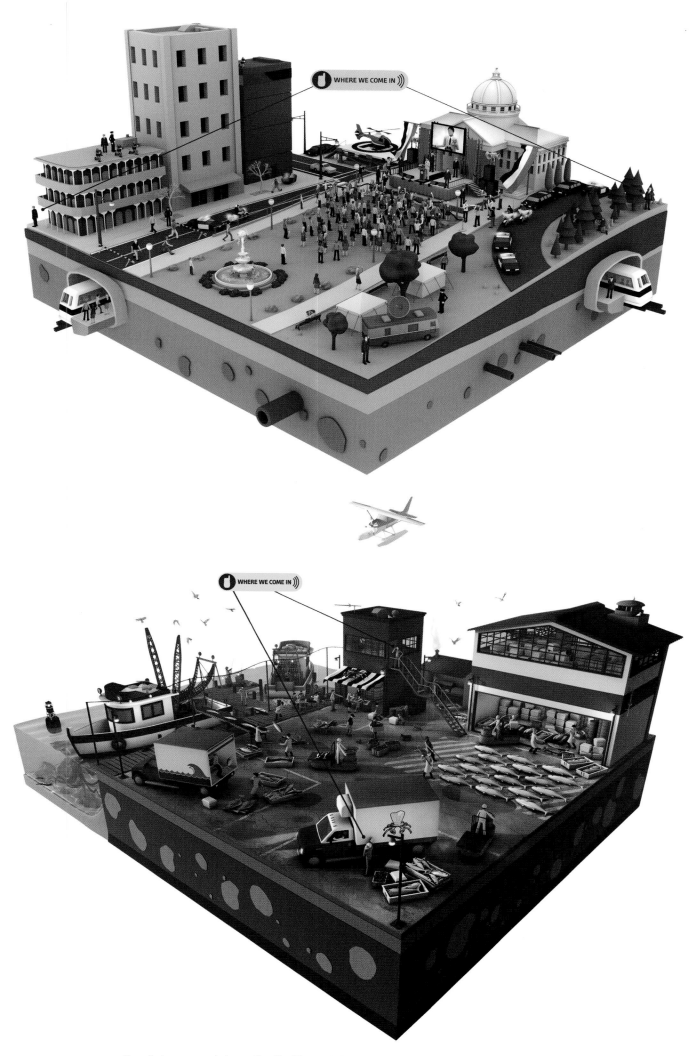

WHERE WE COME IN)))

WHERE WE COME IN)))

WHERE WE COME IN))

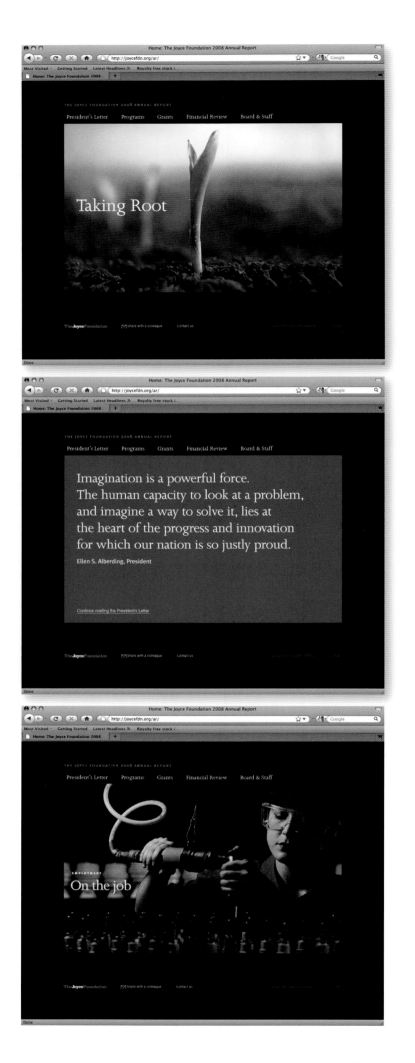

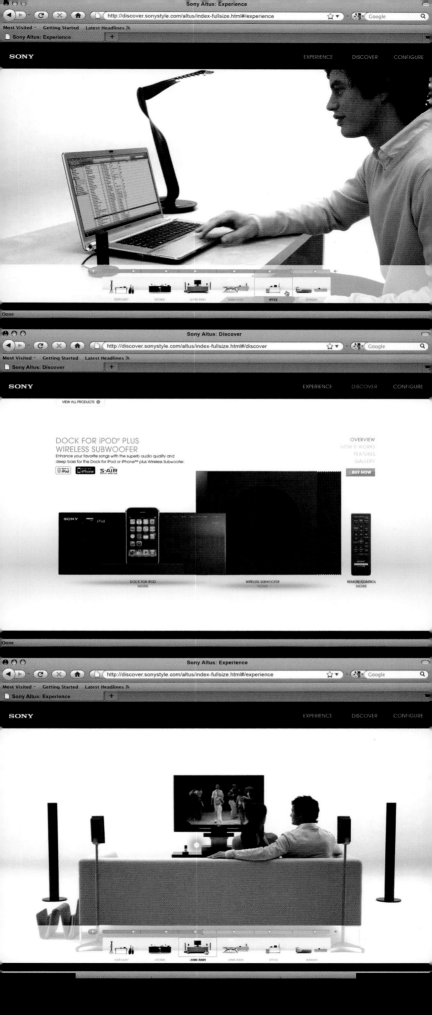

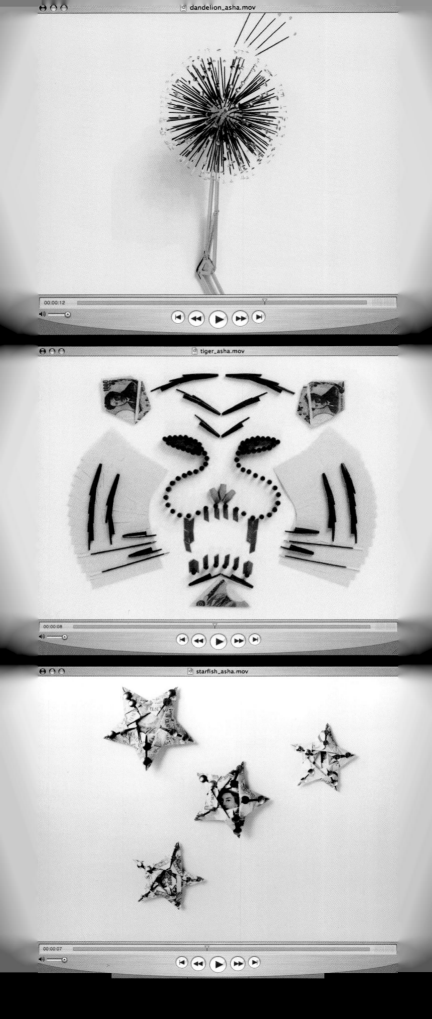

00:00:12

00:00:08

00:00:07

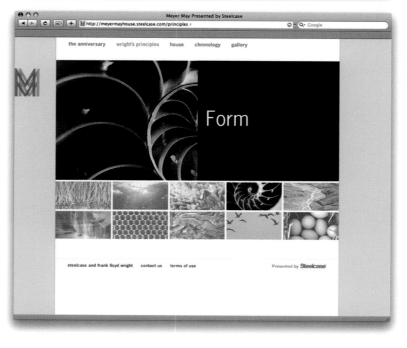

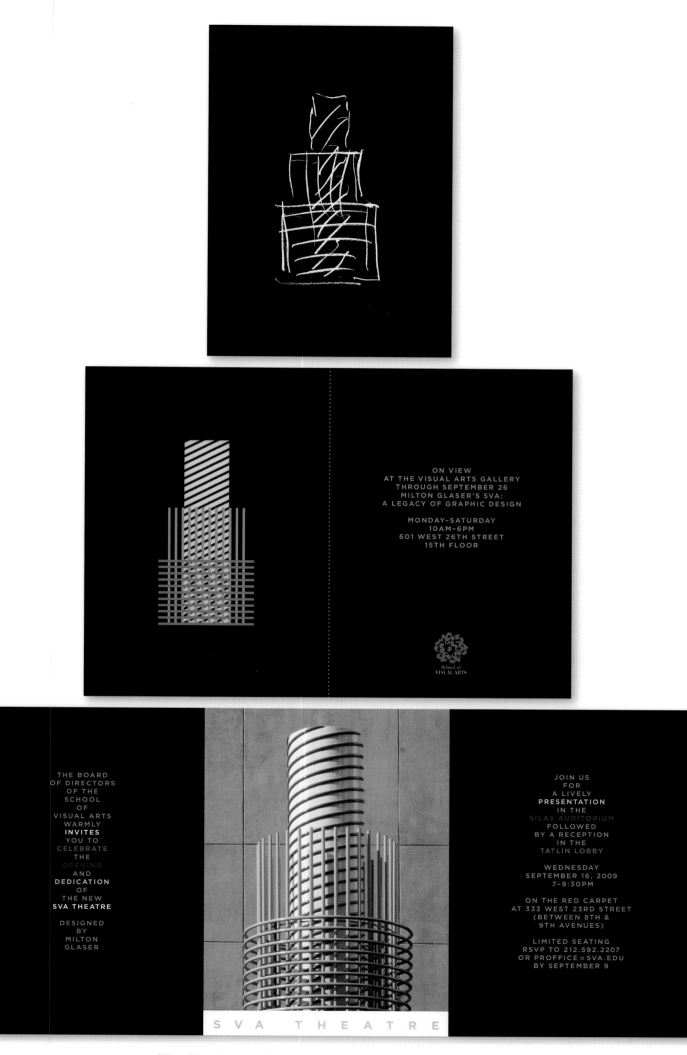

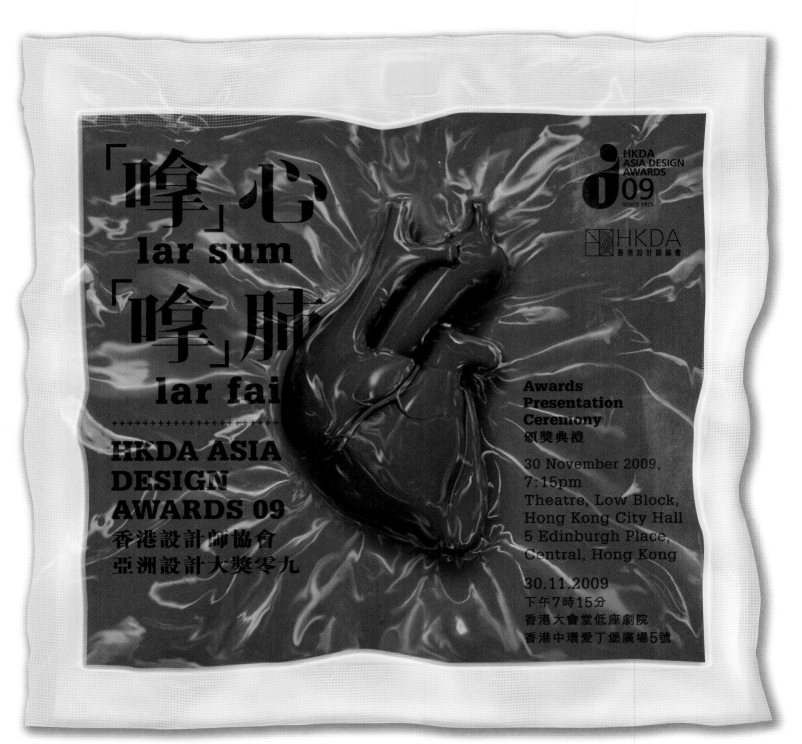

DINAMO
ecoeficiencia
energética

Saavedra Fajardo 7, 1º B
30001 Murcia, España
T +34 968 222 912

www.dinamo.cc

DINAMO
ecoeficiencia
energética

González Adalid 11, 1º D
30001 Murcia, España
T +34 968 222 912

www.dinamo.cc

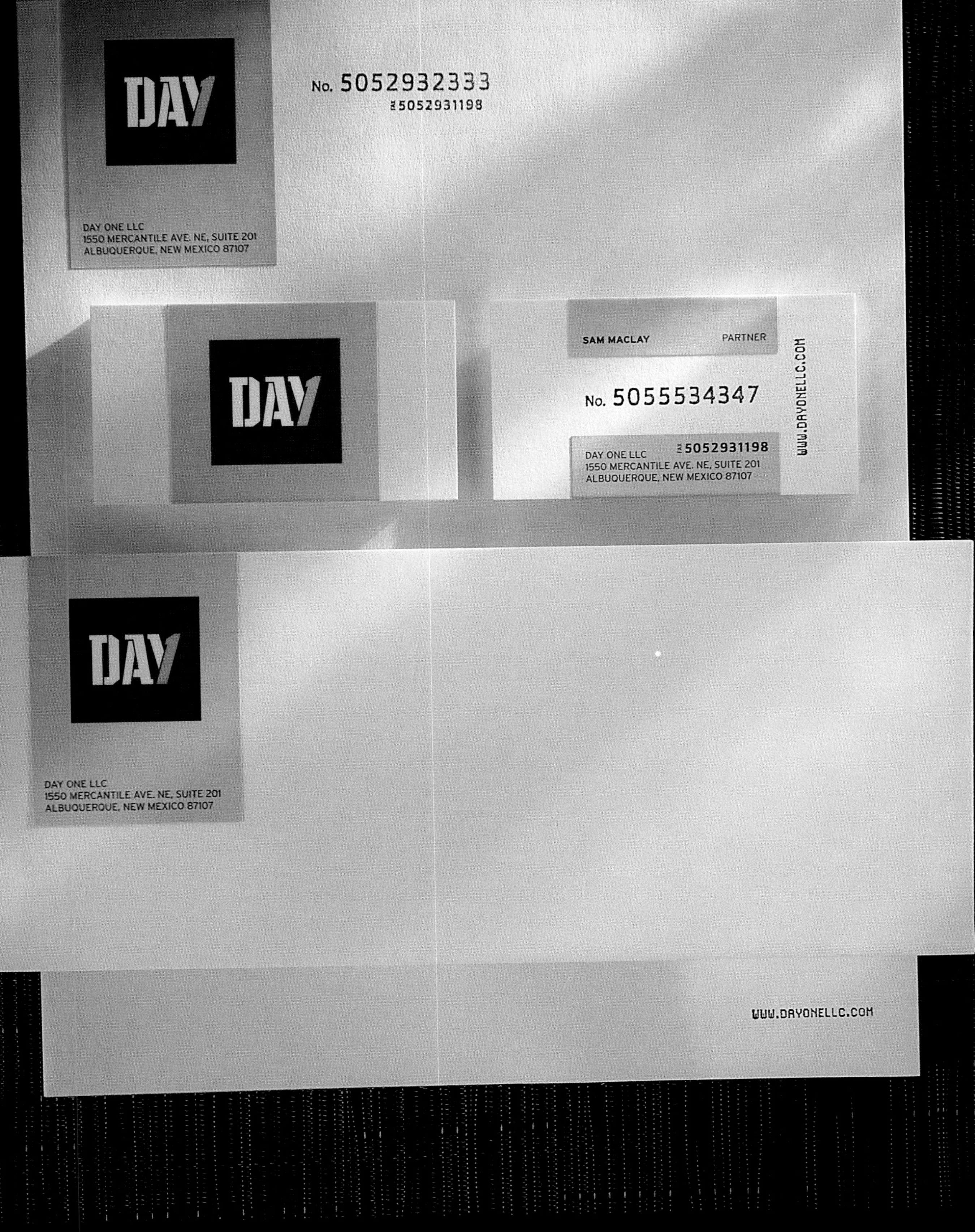

No. 5052932333
5052931198

DAY ONE LLC
1550 MERCANTILE AVE. NE, SUITE 201
ALBUQUERQUE, NEW MEXICO 87107

SAM MACLAY   PARTNER

No. 5055534347

DAY ONE LLC   5052931198
1550 MERCANTILE AVE. NE, SUITE 201
ALBUQUERQUE, NEW MEXICO 87107

WWW.DAYONELLC.COM

DAY ONE LLC
1550 MERCANTILE AVE. NE, SUITE 201
ALBUQUERQUE, NEW MEXICO 87107

WWW.DAYONELLC.COM

OAKLAND

OF NASHVILLE, TN

Martin Williams www.martinwilliams.com | **MIMA**
Wall-to-Wall Studios www.walltowall.com | **Oakland Community Council**
Ventress Design Group, Inc. www.ventress.com | **Gubbins Light and Power Company**
Yonalee Design www.jeenaya.com | **Saveurs D'ailleurs**

HONEY

?*!!ock

SAN ANSELMO PUBLIC LIBRARY
AND HISTORICAL MUSEUM

ihu

kru khmer

POLLOCK Alberta, Canada | **Keli Pollock**
Yonalee Design www.yonalee.com | **Kuka Escapes**
Michael Schwab Studio www.michaelschwab.com | **San Anselmo Public Library**
Saatchi Design Worldwide www.saatchi.co.nz | **Ihu**
Graphaus www.graphaus.com | **Kru Khmer** | Logos **172**

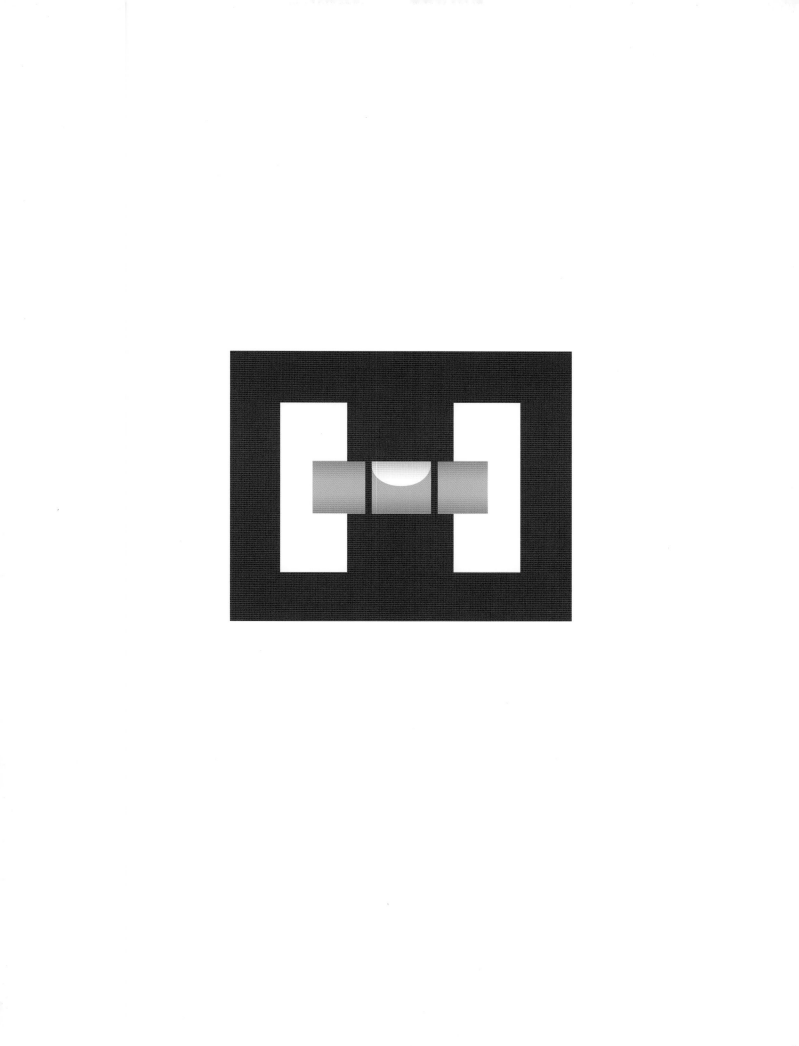

Concussion LLP www.concussion.net | **ExpoTurf**
RLR Advertising & Marketing www.rlradvertising.com | **Bikewerks**
ARGUS, LLC www.argussf.com | **BRIDGE Housing Corporation**
Michael Schwab Studio www.michaelschwab.com | **Angels & Cowboys, Inc**
Siegel+Gale www.siegelgale.com | **Qualcomm** | Logos **175**

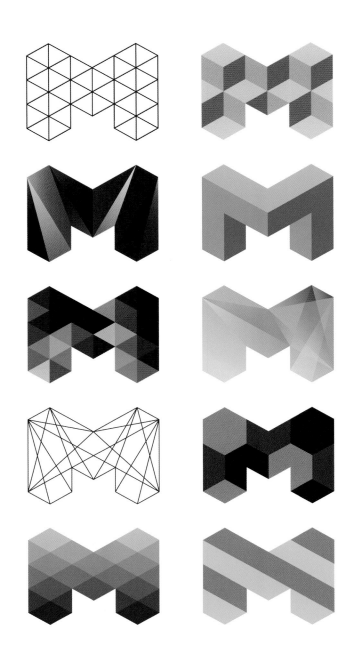

Michael Doret/Alphabet Soup Type Founders www.michaeldoret.com | **Simstan Music, Ltd.**
MiresBall, Inc. www.miresball.com | **Lux Art Institute**
Mangos www.mangosinc.com | **Maxfield Gast**
MiresBall, Inc. www.miresball.com | **Lux Art Institute** | MusicCDs **179**

PITTYVAICH
SPEYSIDE
SINGLE MALT SCOTCH WHISKY
NATURAL CASK STRENGTH
Estº 1975
PERHAPS THE SHORTEST LIVED OF ALL SPEYSIDE DISTILLERIES, PITTYVAICH WAS BUILT IN 1975 AS A PARTNER FOR NEARBY DUFFTOWN. THE NAME IS GAELIC & MAY REFER TO AN EARLY DWELLING ON THE SITE, A 'FARMSTEAD AT THE BIRCH WOOD'. NESTLING NEAR RED DEER COUNTRY IN THE DULLAN GLEN, PITTYVAICH DREW PROCESS WATER FROM TWO SPRINGS, CONVALLEYS & BALLIEMORE, & OPERATED FOR JUST 18 YEARS UNTIL CLOSING IN 1993. SO YOU COULD SAY THAT THE INTRIGUING & RARE LIMITED EDITION MALT WHISKY IN THIS BOTTLE, DISTILLED IN 1989, IS OLDER THAN THE DISTILLERY FROM WHICH IT CAME. VERY FRESH FOR ITS AGE & APPETISINGLY CRISP, CLEAN & GRASSY, IT MAKES A FINE, SWEET-NATURED & DELIGHTFULLY UNUSUAL APERITIF.
BOTTLE Nº 5373 ONE OF 6000
20
YEAR OLD
LIMITED EDITION DISTILLED 1989
DUFFTOWN, SPEYSIDE
PRODUCED & BOTTLED IN SCOTLAND
57.5% vol 70cl/700ml ℮
PITTYVAICH
SPEYSIDE
SINGLE MALT SCOTCH WHISKY
PERHAPS THE SHORTEST LIVED OF ALL SPEYSIDE DISTILLERIES, PITTYVAICH WAS BUILT IN 1975 AS A PARTNER FOR NEARBY DUFFTOWN. THE NAME IS GAELIC & MAY REFER TO AN EARLY DWELLING ON THE SITE, A 'FARMSTEAD AT THE BIRCH WOOD'. NESTLING NEAR RED DEER COUNTRY IN THE DULLAN GLEN, PITTYVAICH DREW PROCESS WATER FROM TWO SPRINGS, CONVALLEYS & BALLIEMORE, & OPERATED FOR JUST 18 YEARS UNTIL CLOSING IN 1993. SO YOU COULD SAY THAT THE INTRIGUING & RARE LIMITED EDITION MALT WHISKY IN THIS BOTTLE, DISTILLED IN 1989, IS OLDER THAN THE DISTILLERY FROM WHICH IT CAME. VERY FRESH FOR ITS AGE & APPETISINGLY CRISP, CLEAN & GRASSY, IT MAKES A FINE, SWEET-NATURED & DELIGHTFULLY UNUSUAL APERITIF.
LIMITED BOTTLING ONE OF 6000
LIMITED EDITION DISTILLED 1989
DUFFTOWN, SPEYSIDE
PRODUCED & BOTTLED IN SCOTLAND
57.5% vol 70cl/700ml ℮

MICHAEL VANDERBYL REINVENT A DESIGN EXHIBITION

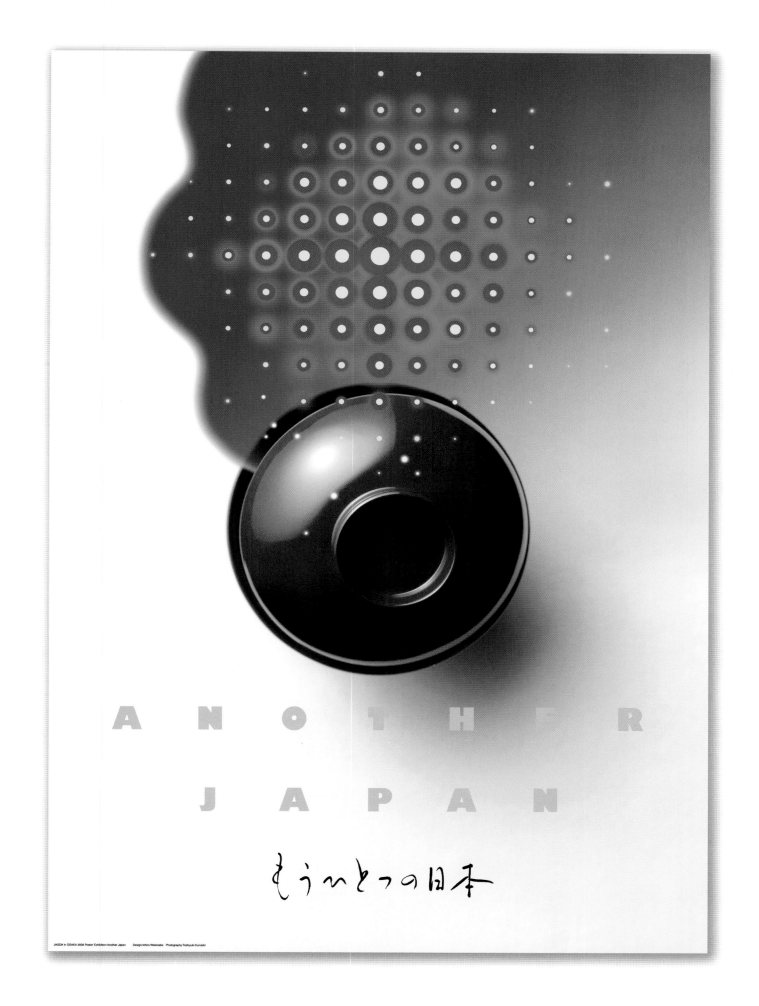

ANOTHER

JAPAN

もうひとつの日本

SAN FRANCISCO JEWISH FILM FESTIVAL 29

JULY 23–AUGUST 10
SFJFF.ORG/866-55-TICKETS
SF/CASTRO/JULY 23–30
SF/JCCSF/AUGUST 8–9
BERKELEY/AUGUST 1–8
PALO ALTO/AUGUST 1–6
SAN RAFAEL/AUGUST 8–10

PRESENTING SPONSORS   MEDIA SPONSORS
Blue Angel WELLS FARGO   abc7 KGO-TV-DT EAST BAY EXPRESS GUARDIAN HeeB indieWIRE J. 91.7 KALW 102.1 KDFC KQED MOBILE COMMONS SFSTATION yelp

DESIGN: VOLUME INC./volumesf.com

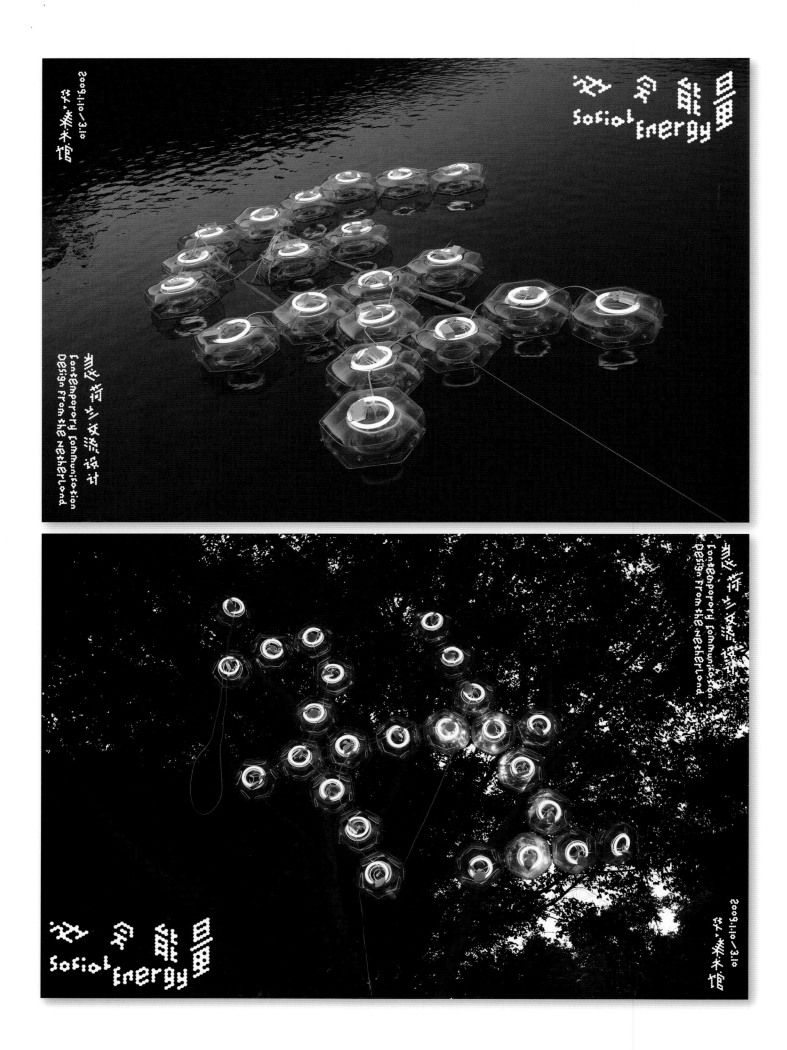

Varnish

Available in gloss, satin and dull finishes, varnish is essentially ink without pigment, so it can be run using a regular unit on the press and hold exact dot-for-dot registration. A gloss varnish deepens colors on a printed piece, while satin and dull finishes reduce contrast. For overall protection and sheen, varnish is flooded onto the entire sheet. One drawback of varnish is that it tends to yellow over time, becoming most evident in unprinted areas. Printers also have to use a spray powder to keep printed sheets from sticking together while the varnish is still wet. This may leave a faint residue. Still, varnish offers opportunities to elicit a variety of dramatic design effects at a relatively inexpensive cost.

6 | MCCOY SILK

Inline dull varnish + drytrapped dot-for-dot gloss varnish on lip highlights   Inline tinted satin varnish / Conventional four-color process

3 The Standard

sappi

A Sappi Guide to Designing for Print: Tips, Techniques and Methods for Achieving Optimum Printing Results

Varnish & Coatings

Coatings

Press coatings come in two types – aqueous and UV. Aqueous looks and performs much like varnish, but provides better rub protection and does not yellow over time. Its 60-70% water content makes flood coating the preferred use, although spot coating is possible using a Cyrel plate. Unlike varnish, aqueous dries quickly, allowing for faster back-ups, but it does require the use of heavier stock (60lb. text and up) to avoid paper curl when wet. On the other hand, UV coating is nearly all solids and cures instantly under ultraviolet light. More protective than aqueous, UV provides an exceptional gloss level, accepts a wider range of specialty techniques, and works well on any type of stock. UV also lends itself to spot applications. One caution: UV's high-solids level is vulnerable to cracking, so special care must be taken during curing and in the bindery.

Ten
Ideas
that
Matter

Forty
Designers
who saw
a way to
change
the world

One
Paper
Company
who
believed
in their
vision

sappi

ASSIGNMENT
#TV: 4825
CLIENT
Aspen Valley
Ranch
ASPEN, COLORADO

ASSIGNMENT
#TV: 4835
CLIENT
The Junior
League of Houston
'PEACE MEALS' COOKBOOK

ASSIGNMENT
#TV: 4798
CLIENT
The Hyatt,
Lost Pines
BASTROP, TEXAS

ASSIGNMENT
#TV: 4837
CLIENT
Boot Ranch
FREDRICKSBURG,
TEXAS

ASSIGNMENT
#TV: 4791
CLIENT
The European Villages
at The Landmark
GREENWOOD VILLAGE, CO

ASSIGNMENT
#TV: 4758
CLIENT
Capella
Pedregal
CABO SAN LUCAS, MEXICO

Aspen Valley Ranch is a luxury lifestyle development being created within an 831-acre working ranch. Arriving the first day with a shot list and a compressed schedule, we found a dilapidated barn, amazing vistas, incredible light and little else. With the help of Chad, the ranch foreman, we began bringing the developer's vision to life. Well-used saddles suggested a tack room. A glowing bonfire on a mountaintop became a campout at trail's end. Family, friends, ranch hands and local cowboys became the authentic faces evoking a timeless way of life.

The world is full of stories

Some fade from memory as soon as they are told while others live on and are remembered for ages.

How many stories do you know?

WHAT IS THE STORY?

WHAT IS THE STORY?

What's your story? Pictures are worth a thousand words and we want to help you tell your tale with the impact it deserves.

Please contact us to learn more about the story behind this book and how we can be a critical part of your communication strategy.

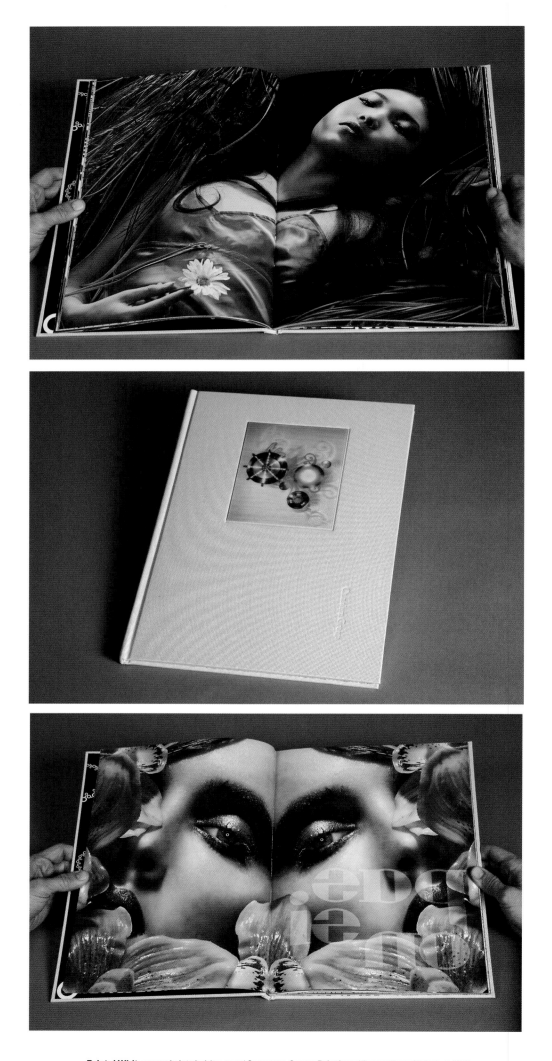

Unrivalled
reproduction —
Now with
vegetable inks.

To find out more
call Phil Le Monde
or Gary Bird on
020 7729 0091
or visit us online at
gavinmartin.co.uk

Gavin Martin Associates Limited

NEWS SO GOOD. YOU MAY
NOT WANT TO SHARE IT.

CARIBOU COFFEE.

The function of the artist is to express reality as *felt*. Robert Motherwell

ABSTRACT EXPRESSIONISTS

The abstract expressionists revolutionized art and moved the U.S. to the center of the international art scene during the 1940s and 1950s. Based primarily in New York City, this group of artists with radically different styles created a new visual language based on color, motion, and the expression of universal truths. In the process, they transformed the act of painting into a means of self-discovery, which was both uniquely American and utterly new.

Hans Hofmann   44 USA

Willem de Kooning   44 USA

Mark Rothko   44 USA

Jackson Pollock   44 USA

Arshile Gorky   44 USA

Clyfford Still   44 USA

Robert Motherwell   44 USA

Joan Mitchell   44 USA

Adolph Gottlieb   44 USA

Barnett Newman   44 USA

Howard E. Paine Virginia, United States | **United States Postal Service**
Derry Noyes Washington D.C., United States | **United States Postal Service**
Derry Noyes Washington D.C., United States | **United States Postal Service** | **Stamps 227**

JUSTICES OF THE SUPREME COURT OF THE UNITED STATES

NEGRO LEAGUES BASEBALL | NEGRO LEAGUES BASEBALL

RUBE FOSTER

Howard E. Paine Virginia, United States | United States Postal Service
Derry Noyes Washington D.C., United States | United States Postal Service

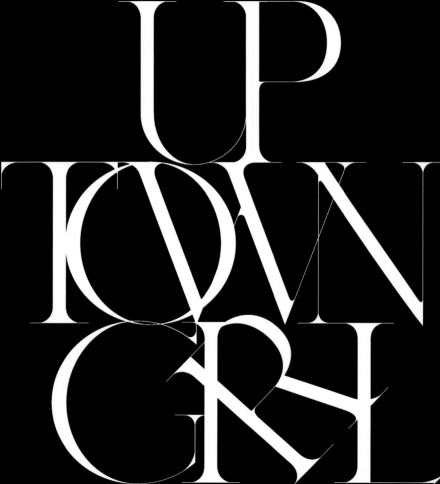

Credits&Comments

AnnualReports

18 Neenah Paper 2008 Annual Report | Design Firm: Addison, New York | Creative Director: Richard Colbourne | Design Director: Jason Miller | Illustrators: Raymond Biesinger, Mario Hugo, ilovedust, Faiyaz Jafri, Aakash Nihalani | Paper Type: Various Neenah Fine Paper Stocks | Photographers: Sarah Illenberger, Dean Kaufman, Horacio Salinas, Corriette Schoenaerts | Print Producer: Georgiann Baran | Print Run: 19,000 copies | Project Manager: Michelle Steg Faranda | Writer: Edward Nebb | Client: Neenah Paper

Description: Neenah Paper's directive to us was to communicate all the ways in which the company had executed its strategic plan in becoming a more focused and agile fine paper company. The annual report needed to express both the specialized niche focus of Neenah's products and culture as well as the straightforward accountability of their strategic planning and execution. We found that in many ways, the qualities that made Neenah a more interesting and competitive company, also positioned them strongly to weather the economic downturn. We developed a typographic solution, based on a series of terms that communicate these differentiators—which are simple and direct—and then executed the typography in unique and surprising ways, relevant to each topic. It is very straightforward in message, yet at the same time highly expressive from a visual standpoint.

19 Gensler Annual Report 2009 | Design Firm: Gensler, San Francisco | Art Director: Mark Coleman | Designers: Mark Jones, Tiffany Ricardo | Editor: John Parman | Client: Gensler

Description: Gensler's annual report provides an overview of the firm's year, noting exemplary design and community service accomplishments, along with firm and practice area developments. The report is distributed to all Gensler staff, clients, consultants and friends to celebrate the firm's annual achievements in building communities.

20 NMB 75 | Design Firm: Design Army, Washington | Creative Director: Jake Lefebure, Pum Lefebure | Designer: Taylor Buckholz | Client: National Mediation Board

Description: The National Mediation Board (NMB), established by the 1934 amendments to the Railway Labor Act of 1926, is an independent agency that performs a central role in facilitating harmonious labor-management relations within two of the nation's key transportation modes—the railroads and airlines. The 2009 Annual Report marked the 75th Anniversary for the NMB and we set out to create an annual that takes a look back at the airline and railway industries since 1934, and prior. The use of archive images set the tone for the annual, while bold color overlays bring the images in to the current timeframe. Icons and other design elements are added for graphic flair, and the cover gets a silver foil emboss to celebrate the National Mediation Board's achievements.

21 CSPD 2009 Annual Report | Design Firm: WAX, Calgary | Art Director: Jonathan Herman | Creative Director: Monique Gamache, Joe Hospodarec | Photographer: Justen Lacoursiere | Writer: Tim Anderson | Client: Calgary Society for Persons with Disabilities

22 Hold Fast | Design Firm: Mangos, Malvern | Associate Creative Directors: Justin Moll, Charles Smolover | Chief Creative Officer: Bradley Gast | Creative Director: Joanne de Menna | Print Producer: Susan Trickel | Project Manager: Patti Monaco | Client: Harbor Point

Description: Harbor Point is a reinsurance company that adheres to a core set of business principles. For their 2008 Annual Report, we used a nautical theme to present these ideas, in the form of a weathered guide for sailors entitled, "Hold Fast."

AwardAnnuals

23 Philadelphia Design Awards Catalog | Design Firm: gdloftPHL, Philadelphia | Art Director: Allan Espiritu | Designers: Matt Bednarik, Christian Mortlock, Mike Sung Park | Editor: Joseph Schiavo | Writer: Michele Cooper | Client: AIGA Philadelphia

Description: The project is a catalog design for American Institute of Graphic Arts, Philadelphia Design Competition. In the preliminary stages of the catalog, gdloft focused on representing all designs, winners or not, as well as creating a book to serve as "art" within the context of a gallery (for the winners exhibition). The catalog print-run was limited to the same amount of entries received (576) to represent all the work of the design community. Using a variable printing program, each cover is a different color of a predetermined spectrum; thus, making each catalog entirely unique no two pieces are identical. In addition, each catalog was individually numbered. When all the catalogs are stacked together the spines create a seamless spectrum of color that produces the quality of a sculpture.

24, 25 AIGA Boston 25th Anniversary Book | Design Firm: Stoltze Design, Boston | Art Director: Clifford Stoltze | Designers: Robert Beerman, Kyle Nelson, Lauren Vajda | Client: AIGA Boston

Awards

26, 27 The Creative Promise Certificate | Design Firm: Sagmeister, Inc., New York | Creative Director: Stefan Sagmeister | Designer: Joe Shouldice | Print Producer: Blackbooks Stencils | Client: The Vilcek Foundation

Description: This certificate is comprised of three layers of intricately laser-diecut paper. When hung for display the neon orange backside of the paper reflects on itself and the wall making appear as though it is glowing.

Books

28, 29 Columbia Abstract 2007/2008 | Design Firm: Sagmeister, Inc., New York | Creative Director: Stefan Sagmeister | Designers: Daniel Harding, Joe Shouldice, Richard The | Editor: Scott Marble | Client: Graduate School of Architecture, Planning and Preservation

Description: Columbia University asked the studio to design their annual publication Abstract, a yearbook for the Graduate School of Architecture, Planning and Preservation. The content is divided into three different color-coded books which insert into each other to form their own pyramid-shaped architecture. The smallest book contains only photos of staff and students, the middle book contains only text and the large book showcases all the student work. An extensive cross-reference system directs users to related content between the books.

30 Ninth Letter Volume 6 Issue 1 | Design Firm: fame-fame studio, Champaign | Art Director: Jimmy Luu | Designers: Nate Baltikas, Tanya Bounroueng, Christine Jeng, Bryan Kveton, Darren McPherson | Photographer: Lauren Ayers | Senior Designer: Huang Li, Adam Muran | Client: University of Illinois

Description: This issue is the first issue after Ninth Letter's re-design. The format size was decreased and the text-image relationship changed to encourage a more open-interpretive reading experience. The supplements offer visual interpretations of the literature, but each supplement doesn't necessarily go with one single story. The opening titles for each story include custom typefaces designed for the issue.

31 THE NEXT HUNDRED MILLION | Design Firm: Penguin Group (USA) Inc., New York | Designer: Tal Goretsky | Client: Penguin Group (USA) Inc.

32 +rosebud nr. 7 VERY FUNNY! | Design Firm: Rosebud, Inc., Vienna | Creative Director: Ralf Herms | Client: Rosebud, Inc.

Description: +rosebud is a design magazine that operates with the desire to explore and exhaust the possibilities and potentials that paper and 2D-structure have to offer. The symbolic name, a derivation from the last, mysterious word that the newspaper tycoon stammers out in Orson Welles' film classic "Citizen Kane," figuratively indicates that +rosebud is an attempt to explain the puzzle "medium"—keeping Welles' experimental spirit in mind.

33 Gorgia O'Keeffe Camp Gear | Design Firm: Michael Schwab Studio, San Anselmo | Designer: Michael Schwab | Photographer: Terry Heffernan | Print Producer: Steve Zeifman | Client: Rush Creek Editions

Description: This limited edition box set of fine art prints documents the personal camp gear used by Georgia O'Keeffe on her creative journeys in the desert Southwest.

34 (left) The Resurrectionist | Design Firm: Faceout Studio, Bend | Designer: Charles Brock | Illustrator: Michael Koelsch | Client: Algonquin Books

34 (right) Wine on Tuesdays | Design Firm: Faceout Studio, Bend | Designer: Nate Salciccioli | Photographer: Steve Gardner | Client: Thomas Nelson Publishers

35 Basilique Notre-Dame de Montréal | Design Firm: Dominique Mousseau designer graphique, Montréal | Author: Colette Tougas | Design Director: Dominique Mousseau | Editor: Mario Brodeur | General Director: Yoland Tremblay | Photographer: Normand Rajotte | Print Producer: L'Empreinte | Client: Fabrique de la paroisse Notre-Dame de Montréal

Description: Basilique Notre-Dame de Montréal (Notre-Dame Basilica of Montreal). 216 pages. Published by La Fabrique de la paroisse Notre-Dame de Montréal and directed by Mario Brodeur. This art book dedicated to Tourists, Specialists of Heritage and Religious art, Architects and Art Historians includes: A history of the Basilica told in a convivial tone, with archival images; thirteen entries by specialists documenting the multifaceted institution; an 80-page photographic essay offering unusual perspectives.

36 You Better Not Cry | Design Firm: St. Martin's Press, New York | Designer: Steve Snider | Photographers: Gabe Palmer/Jupiter Images | Client: St. Martin's Press

37 (top left) Courage | Design Firm: St. Martin's Press, New York | Artist: Richard Willis | Designer: Steve Snider | Client: St. Martin's Press

37 (top right) The Manual of Detection | Design Firm: Penguin Group (USA) Inc., New York | Designer: Tal Goretsky | Client: Penguin Group (USA) Inc.

37 (bottom left) A Thread of Sky, (bottom right) There Once Lived a Woman Who Tried To Kill Her Neighbor's Baby | Design Firm: Penguin Group (USA) Inc., New York | Designer: Christopher Brand | Illustrator: Sam Weber | Client: Penguin Group (USA) Inc.

38 C.S. Lewis Signature Classics | Design Firm: Faceout Studio, Bend | Designer: Jason Gabbert | Client: Harper One

39 Darwin's Armada | Design Firm: Faceout Studio, Bend | Designer: Charles Brock | Client: WW Norton

40, 41 The Model as Muse: Embodying Fashion | Design Firm: Matsumoto Inc., New York | Art Director: Takaaki Matsumoto | Designers: Hisami Aoki, Takaaki Matsumoto | Client: The Metropolitan Museum of Art

42 The Harley-Davidson Museum | Design Firm: Shine Advertising, Madison | Art Director: John Krull | Chief Creative Officer: Michael Kriefski | Digital Artist: Chad Bollenbach | Photographer: Jeff Lendrum | Writer: James Breen | Client: Harley Davidson

43 Anish Kapoor: Memory | Design Firm: Matsumoto Inc., New York | Art Director: Takaaki Matsumoto | Designers: Takaaki Matsumoto, Hisami Aoki | Client: Deutsche Guggenheim

44, 45 PLATINUM Kismet Yacht Book | Design Firm: pivot design, inc., Chicago | Designer: Jason Thompson | Executive Creative Director: Brock Haldeman | Client: Kismet Yacht

Description: Kismet is a 225-foot luxury yacht that sails guests through the Mediterranean and the Caribbean. It is ranked 79 on a list of the 100 largest yachts worldwide. This book was designed as a keepsake for passengers to remind them of their experience and the grandeur of the Kismet, and to inspire them to return. Using vivid photography and copy that reflects the idyllic experience, we designed this case-bound book to guide readers through the journey of being onboard.

Branding

46, 47 PLATINUM VONROSEN corporate design | Design Firm: KMS TEAM, Munich | Account Director: Katja Egloff | Art Director: Susana Frau | Creative Directors: Michael Keller, Knut Maierhofer | Designer: Teresa Lehmann | Client: Von Rosen AG & Co. KG

Description: VONROSEN is a Berlin fashion label that distributes its products exclusively via the Internet to a select clientele. The oval signet with the engraved initials of the proprietors functions as an identifying mark for members of the VONROSEN circle. As a graphical code, the signet is translated into all media—as a cross-fading pattern on the webpage, a high-quality foil embossing on the business stationery, or on the cover of the product packaging perforated by innovative laser technology. The formal vocabulary is marked by aesthetic reduction and an urban atmosphere and thus reflects the classic-purist style of the collection.

48, 49 ECHO | Design Firm: SenseTeam, Shenzhen | Creative Director: Yiyang Hei | Designers: Yiyang Hei, Zhao Liu, Ting Zhan, Meng Zhao | Client: Shenzhen Vanke Real Estate Co.,Ltd

Description: This is a exhibition for Shenzhen Vanke Real Estate Co., Ltd. "Beginning of pure life" project's which named "ECHO," which is mainly display natural elements, the exhibition are located in several large-scale commercial plazas. According to the project, the space's design inspiration comes from the natural elements such as water, wind and stone. Therefore you can see lots of stones in the exhibition, "Stones" are not only a information-tion wearer such as panels but one of a display object. "Stones" are cutting in straight-line and have distinct edges and corners. Special hollowing practice make them can put lots of displays and play loop pictures. "Stones" are scattered in the exhibition everywhere. But in front of them, you can see the LED characters of 清林径 and 回声. The overall style of the space design bias modern minimalism, reflect a new concept of: Technology interpret natural.

50, 51 Snog Brand Identity | Design Firm: ico Design Consultancy Ltd, London. | Account Director: Sandra Dartnell | Creative Director: Ben Tomlinson | Designers: Amanda Gaskin, Anand Nagrick | Web Developers: David Ashman, Immo Blaese | Writer: Gerard Ivall | Client: Snog

Description: Snog is the first frozen yogurt brand to hit British shores and Snogging mania is set to sweep the nation. It's an exciting new retail concept with a bold name and brand created by ico. The Snog name, coined by ico, is derived from "Snow & Yogurt" and is the perfect solution for a bold, young, urban and British brand. In effect, the name informed the entire creative concept. A fun and infectious copy-led approach followed. Bright pop colours and an edgy typographic style completed the brand. ico are working with Cinimod Studio on the shop interiors. They combine unusual and innovative elements to create a deliberately quirky, but inviting environment. Cinimod are responsible for the architectural and lighting elements while ico manages the brand across a number of interior applications including interior artworks, a menu lightbox, signage and customer literature. www.ifancyasnog.com

52 Off-Site Records Management Shred Truck Graphics | Design Firm: Gee + Chung Design, San Francisco | Creative Director, Designer, Illustrator: Earl Gee | Client: Off-Site Records Management

Description: The objective of the project was to create graphics for a document destruction truck for an off-site records management company which would convey the function of the truck, and extend the company brand. The solution utilizes truck's two sides to showcase the symbol and company name on each side, using gradation as a metaphor for customers moving their documents "off-site." The logo's dimensional boxes suggest space and storage, forming a circle to represent the access, retrieval and linking of information. The shredder mechanism is highlighted in orange, and engages the viewer by asking, "Have you shredded your confidential records?" The top of the truck functions as a dimensional billboard displaying the firm's complete range of document storage solutions. The back of the truck displays the company's document storage offerings and use bright orange arrows to highlight the shredding bins.

53 Acadia | Design Firm: Interbrand, New York | Associate Creative Director: Mike Knaggs | Chief Creative Officer: Chris Campbell | Creative Director: Alan Roll | Creative Strategists: Jeff Dawson, Miguel Rivera, Lauren Thiele | Designer: Lucy Manlik | Senior Designers: David Hong, Scott Huston, Nao Okawa | Client: Acadia

Description:

Objective – Our clients, EMC, Cisco and VMware had challenged Interbrand to develop a business strategy, name, identity and visual system for their new joint venture into a compelling private cloud computing solution.

Deliverables – Interbrand was to provide the following as well as assist in setting a two phrase launch timetable of development:
a. Business and Market Strategy
b. Naming and Tone of Voice
c. Identity and Visual System
d. Website development for soft launch
e. Animation on website for soft launch

Strategy Solution – The private cloud computing solution is powered by the strong alliance of the three brands and differentiated by providing customers with processes and services to transform their companies to the private cloud. The transformation to the private cloud gave us the bases of the brand's personality attributes of: Expertise / Focus / Passion
This attributes and the idea of providing transformative impact to the private cloud drove the naming and creative exploration.

Naming – Acadia. The name "Acadia" was selected for best capturing the brand attributes. Derived from the Greek Arcadia, meaning pastoral utopia, the name Acadia announces the emergence of a more seamless IT landscape. Amidst all the technological clutter and complexity, Acadia is your bridge to a simpler, more enabling environment.

Creative – The identity, visual solution and tone of voice created express the

brand idea of transforming customers to the private cloud in an impactful manner that is immediately seen in their business. The basis of a predominant use of black for all visuals reflects the stature and expertise of the Acadia. The illustrations represent the journey that customers take with Acadia as their business is transformed from one direction to the next in a passionate and focused manner. The vertical nature and upward motion of the graphic system is also a visual interpretation of transformation to the private cloud. The identity provides the endpoint of success to the journey and illustrates the confidence that the alliance of three companies provide.

54 (top) Greyhound Bus | Design Firm: Butler, Shine, Stern & Partners, Sausalito | Executive Creative Directors: John Butler, Mike Shine | Design Director: Neal Zimmerman | Designer: Ajana Green | Client: Greyhound

Description: In a move to improve the service offering and customer experience, Greyhound introduced new coaches with WiFi, electrical outlets and more legroom. We redesigned the buses to elevate the brand's image. Inspiration came from Greyhound's rich graphic heritage.

54 (bottom) BoltBus | Design Firm: Butler, Shine, Stern & Partners, Sausalito | Executive Creative Directors: John Butler, Mike Shine | Design Director: Neal Zimmerman | Designer: Ajana Green | Client: Greyhound

Description: We named and designed the graphics for Boltbus, a new curb-side carrier in the Northeast equipped with WiFi and electrical outlets. The design is bold and acts like a mobile billboard for the brand.

55 (top) Coca-Cola Summer Cans | Design Firm: Turner Duckworth, San Francisco | Account Director: Jessica Rogers | Art Director: Sarah Moffat | Creative Directors: Bruce Duckworth, David Turner | Designer: Josh Michels, Rebecca Williams | Client: The Coca-Cola Company North America

Description: The Coca-Cola Summer 2009 campaign celebrates the joy and optimism of summer and Coke's authentic connection to the season. The graphics designed by Turner Duckworth were featured on packaging, in-store displays and select TV spots. The designs will also be used for summer premiums on everything from t-shirts and hats to beach towels. Five cans were released overall, culminating with a special July 4th holiday can. The designs also appeared on can packs, 2 liters and 20oz bottles, all in celebration of summer's favorite beverage—Coca-Cola.

55 (bottom) Coca-Cola Summer Identity | Design Firm: Turner Duckworth, San Francisco | Art Director: Sarah Moffat | Creative Directors: Bruce Duckworth, David Turner | Designers: Josh Michels, Rebecca Williams | Client: The Coca-Cola Company North America

Description: The Coca-Cola Summer 2009 campaign celebrates the joy and optimism of summer and Coke's authentic connection to the season. The graphics designed by Turner Duckworth were featured on packaging, in-store displays and select TV spots. The designs will also be used for summer premiums on everything from t-shirts and hats to beach towels. Five cans were released overall, culminating with a special July 4th holiday can. The designs also appeared on can packs, 2 liters and 20oz bottles, all in celebration of summer's favorite beverage—Coca-Cola.

56, 57 New Sheridan Hotel Rebrand | Design Firm: Urban Influence, Seattle | Art Director: Stephanie Frier | Creative Director: Pete Wright | Designers: Dana Deininger, Mike Mates, Chaun Osburn | Programmer: Nate Miller | Client: New Sheridan Hotel

Description: In 1891, four years after Telluride, Colorado was founded, the New Sheridan Hotel was built in classic Victorian style. Over the past few decades, directional changes left the hotel without a clearly defined brand position. Renovations in 2008 created an opportunity for Seattle based design studio, Urban Influence, to address the entire customer experience. The new brand strategy capitalized on the esteemed character of this historic town social hub, while grounding the brand in old world service ideals. The solution called for a distinct tactile experience, focusing on unprecedented attention to detail in every touchpoint. From custom debossed menu systems and embroidered uniforms to brochure maps and decorative to-go cups, the New Sheridan's brand experience evolved to entice and engage the modern day leisure traveler.

58, 59 IBM Smarter Planet Illustrations and Posters | Design Firm: Office, San Francisco | Art Directors: Tom Godici, Jason Schulte, Lew Willig | Chief Creative Officer: Chris Wall | Creative Directors: Tom Godici, Greg Ketchum | Designers: Rob Alexander, Will Ecke, Jason Schulte | Executive Creative Director: Susan Westre | Writers: Rob Jamieson, Greg Ketchum, Mike Wing | Client: Ogilvy & Mather, NY

Description: Office collaborated with Ogilvy & Mather New York to develop a series of ads for IBM's "Smarter Planet" campaign. Each ad covers a different topic, such as energy, food, banking and retail, with an essay about how these areas can be transformed to improve the world. Inspired by IBM's vision to help solve the world's biggest problems, and influenced by Paul Rand's original design vision for the company, Office developed bold, iconic illustrations to help tell each story.

Brochures

60, 61 tvsdesign | Design Firm: Ferreira Design Company, Alpharetta | Creative Director: Lionel Ferreira | Designers: Laura Ferreira, Lionel Ferreira | Photographer: John Grover-Grover Studio | Programmer: Daniel Crowder-Monumental | Web Developer: Monumental | Writer: Bill Wittland/Vox Strategic | Client: tvsdesign

Description: Re-branding for an international architecture firm that wanted to re-position for the future, based on reaching a younger creative audience while building on their design sensitive heritage.

Credits&Comments

62, 63 feno brochure | Design Firm: KMS TEAM, Munich | Account Director: Sandra Ehm | Art Director: Patrick Märki | Creative Directors: Michael Keller, Knut Maierhofer | Designers: Claire Chiquet, May Kato | Print Producers: Christina Baur, Anja Wilzek | Project Manager: Julia Sadlo | Client: feno GmbH

Description: The corporate design reflects feno's holistic approach: The shape of the superposed letters of the key visual element evoke the printed circuits of lighting technology products. The artistic abstractness at the same time refers to the aesthetic perception of complex light installations. Feno's working motto, "before light and beyond," is reflected throughout in the brochure both visually and in terms of content. Technology and aesthetics are juxtaposed on every page of the brochure. The key visual element is featured impressively by the translucent pages.

64 Asia Security Initiative | Design Firm: Methodologie, Seattle | Account Director: Erina Malarkey | Creative Directors: Dale Hart, Anne Traver | Creative Strategist: Anne Traver | Designer: Minh Nguyen | Editor: Paula Thurman | Print Run: Fox Printing | Client: The John D. and Catherine T. MacArthur Foundation

65 Edmiston Charter Directory 2010 | Design Firm: Steven Taylor & Associates, London | Art Director: Steven Taylor | Client: Edmiston & Company

66, 67 Kizashi Brochure | Design Firm: SHR Perceptual Management, Paradise Valley | Art Director: Felix Avina | Client: SHR Perceptual Management

68, 69 Lux Art Institute Newletters | Design Firm: MiresBall, Inc., San Diego | Creative Director: John Ball | Designers: Ashley Kerns, Jason Moll | Senior Designers: Beth Folkerth, Gale Spitzley | Writer: David Fried | Client: Lux Art Institute

70 SMS olive oil | Design Firm: STUDIO INTERNATIONAL, Zagreb | Art Director, Designer: Boris Ljubicic | Photographer: Ivo Pervan | Print Producer: STUDIO INTERNATIONAL | Client: SMS food factory

Description: SMS Olive oil brochure is designed as pages from nature. Olive leaves on the edge of the book are part of SMS logo, manufacturer of olive oil.

71 The Joule hotel identity and collateral | Design Firm: Mirko Ilic Corp, New York | Art Director: Mirko Ilic | Designers: Mirko Ilic, Jee-eun Lee | Client: The Joule

Calendars

72 Topless Calendar | Design Firm: Mytton Williams Ltd., Bath | Creative Director: Bob Mytton | Designer: Keith Hancox | Paper Type: 200gsm, Cover & body text: HannoArt Gloss; 540gsm, Back cover: Colourplan Fuschia Pink | Photographer: Stephen Seal | Print Producer: Keith Lunt | Client Mytton Williams Ltd

Description: The Topless Calendar is Mytton William's annual take on the calendar format. Each year a different format is produced. The design team have an open brief and the project is intended as a surprise gift for clients as well as a talking point to promote the firm's creative services. Mytton Williams worked with photographer Stephen Seal to create 12 highly polished seasonal images of inanimate objects minus their tops. The copy combined with a gloss paper stock and black packaging give the finished article the initial look feel of a top shelf publication, although of course on closer inspection the content is considerably less risqué.

73 X-Ray Calender | Design Firm: Bailey Lauerman, Lincoln | Art Director: Ron Sack | Creative Director: Carter Weitz | Designer: Brandon Oltman | Print Producer: Gayle Adams | Writer: Jim Watson | Client: Barnhart Press

Description: X-Ray Calendar for Barnhart Press. X-Rays are printed on actual x-ray stock for each of the 12 months.

74 Create a beautiful image | Design Firm: ando bv, Den Haag | Design Director: Edwin van Praet | Designer: Yu Zhao | Print Producer: Fokko Tamminga | Client: ando bv

Description: With this Ando agenda you are presented with beautiful images as seen through a kaleidoscope. Each week a new item is showed and inspires curiosity and creative thinking, as it invites you to see the beauty in everyday objects which is hidden inside the book. The agenda also allows you space to create your own week, so you can be as flexible with your dates as the images of a kaleidoscope are.

75 Agency Ham Calendar | Design Firm: Colle + McVoy, Minneapolis | Account Director: Chelsea Chung | Art Director: Jenn Lindeman | Creative Director: Nina Orezzoli | Designer, Web Developer: Brice Hemmer | Executive Creative Director: Mike Caguin | Photographer: Chris Peters | Writer: Jenny Kirmis | Client: Colle + McVoy

Description: More than 13 "pin-up boys" from ad agency Colle+McVoy are featured in the "Agency Ham" calendar with humorous and introspective spreads that reveal the creative and entertaining side of each subject. All proceeds from the sale of each calendar went to charities.

Catalogues

76, 77 PLATINUM Nocturne Brochure | Design Firm: David Sutherland Inc, Rockwall | Art Director: Melissa Englert | Creative Director: Tom Nynas | Photographers: Tom Nynas, John Wong, Ka Yeung | Client: David Sutherland, Inc.

Description: This brochure was used as marketing collateral for two of David Sutherland Inc.'s companies (Sutherland and Perennials) at the 2009 Maison Objet show in Paris. The two companies manufacture fine outdoor furniture and fabrics, respectively. Both the brochure and the companies' booth at the show were themed "Nocturne." The concept was to take a peek at the lives of these outdoor furnishings at night, after everybody goes to sleep. What we found out is that these furnishings spend their evenings with the creatures of the night. A good portion of the photography for this oversize (16" x 20") brochure was accomplished with over several nights with an infrared trail camera. The wait was worthwhile, as eventually we captured several images of nocturnal visitors to our pieces and fabrics.

78, 79 Design Within Reach Tabloid | Design Firm: Morla Design, San Francisco | Art Director: Jennifer Morla, Michael Sainato | Creative Director: Jennifer Morla | Designers: Jennifer Morla, Tina Yuan | Writer: Gwendolyn Horton-Griscom | Client: Design Within Reach

Description: DWR's February Workspace Tabloid was purposefully designed to be a break from the traditional perfect bound catalogs. Considerably less expensive to produce, the oversized format was printed roto-gravure on newsprint creating an accessible, surprising, and cost-effective solution that could reach an expanded prospecting demographic.

80 Handsome Cycles Brochure | Design Firm: Periscope, Minneapolis | Art Director: Kent Bishop | Designer: Jessica Hall Burns | Models: Moustache Jim, Robin Pfeifer | Photographer: Dave Thomas Markley | Photographer's Assistants: David Sweeney, Charles Vaughan | Client: Handsome Cycles

Description: The Handsome Introductory brochure leads with timeless imagery and emotive words to tap into our audiences' love of cycling. While most start-ups are arriving with single page spec sheets filled with geometry, we chose to communicate that a Handsome Cycle is one consumers could not only fall in love with but afford. More than images and words on the page, this brochure communicated the commitment of the new company to create a book that had the weight and printing quality of an established brand.

81 Holts Women's Fall 2009 Brochure | Design Firm: Concrete Design Communication, Toronto | Designer: Leticia Luna | Client: Holt Renfrew

Description: Holt Renfrew is Canada's leading luxury fashion retailer. Its catalogue, Holts, is the retailer's flagship marketing vehicle. Holts combines studio and situational photography shot on location in Paris, Newfoundland and Toronto.

82, 83 CATALOG / 25 | Design Firm: Design Army, Washington | Creative Directors: Pum Lefebure, Jake Lefebure | Designer: Lucas Badger | Photographer: Taran Z | Client: Karla Colletto

Description: Each season Karla Colletto needs to reinvent her line of swimsuits to keep up with the ever-changing fashion industry. The challenge is to make the new line marketable and memorable to purchasers, retailers, and to the magazine community. In 2009 it marked 25 years for the designer and we needed to make a splash. We proposed retrospective look at past lines and designs over 25 years; but given the economic downturn we had to be resourceful. Having half the budget we normally have, we proposed look book at twice the size as previous years. To save money we opted to work with cheap talent (mannequins) and shoot in a small studio in Washington DC. While it took over 5 days to style and shoot all the images, the end result was well worth it.

84 2010 Custom Vehicles Operations Motorcycles | Design Firm: VSA Partners, Inc, Chicago | Account Director: Melissa Schwister | Creative Director: Dana Arnett | Design Director: Luke Galambos | Writer: Joe Grimberg | Client: Harley-Davidson

85 Product Guide 2009 | Design Firm: Ferreira Design Company, Alpharetta | Creative Director: Lionel Ferreira | Designers: Lionel Ferreira, Laura Ferreira | Photographers: Geoff Knight | Client: Tandus

Description: NeoCon trade show product guide showcasing new and established carpet patterns

86, 87 Setu preview piece | Design Firm: mono, Minneapolis | Photographers: Simon Hoegsberg, Jason Lazarus, Cameron Wittig, Chris Sheehan, Christopher Barrett | Client: Herman Miller

Description: Herman Miller asked mono to create a launch piece for its new chair, Setu, at NeoCon World's Trade Fair in Chicago. Herman Miller's one and only mandatory: Make it craveable. Our solution? We identified the strategic tenets of the chair and commissioned three different photographers to deliver their artistic interpretations. The result? A range of distinctly different styles, each working together to create one cohesive brand story. It's a hard-working marketing piece that presents itself as artwork. Each chair benefit blends seamlessly into each photographer's vision and photo narrative. The photography is striking. The design epitomizes the beauty of simplicity. And the writing poetically guides and informs the reader, rather than pitching features and benefits.

88 Edge of Elsewhere | Design Firm: Boccalatte, Sydney | Creative Director: Suzanne Boccalatte | Client: Campbelltown Arts Centre

Description: An exhibition catalogue for a major three-year project that brings together some of the most exciting contemporary artists from across Australia, Asia and the Pacific to develop new artworks in partnership with Sydney communities.

89 Traver Gallery Chihuly Mercurio | Design Firm: Methodologie, Seattle | Creative Director, Creative Strategist: Anne Traver | Designer: Goretti Kao | Photographer: David Emery | Project Manager: Erina Malarkey | Writer: Mark McDonnell | Printer: ColorGraphics | Client: The Traver Gallery

DesignerPromotions

90, 91 The Brand Created by Design | Design Firm: Shin Matsunaga Design Inc., Tokyo | Art Director: Shin Matsunaga | Designer: Shin Matsunaga, Shinjiro Matsunaga, Kensuke Sakakibara, Moemi Kiyokawa | Client: ISSIMBOW, Inc.

92 PLATINUM A Lean Year | Design Firm: Alt Group, Auckland | Creative Director: Dean Poole | Designers: Aaron Edwards, Tony Proffit | Client: Alt Group

Description: The goal was to create a gift for clients celebrating the end of 2009—one of the worst years in global economic history. The solution was found in a cleanskin bottle of wine that both personified its contents and was a testament to the past twelve months—a post-apocalyptic reminder of sorts. Each bottle was slumped, filled and corked by hand.

93 Webster Design Associates Drummer Ploy | Design Firm: Webster Design Associates, Omaha | Art Director: Sean Heisler | Creative Director: Dave Webster | Client: Webster Design Associates

94 TD Ameritrade Fly Away With TDA | Design Firm: Webster Design Associates, Omaha | Art Director: Sean Heisler | Creative Director: Dave Webster | Client: TD Ameritrade

95 Pentagram Papers 39: SIGNS | Design Firm: Pentagram Design, Austin | Art Director: DJ Stout | Client: Pentagram Design

Description: Promotional book for Pentagram to raise awareness and funds for Mobile Loaves and Fishes.

Editorial

96 (top) Lebron James | Design Firm: GQ, New York | Design Director: Fred Woodward | Designer: Thomas Alberty | Client: GQ

96 (bottom) Never Forget | Design Firm: GQ, New York | Design Director: Fred Woodward | Designer: Thomas Alberty | Client: GQ

97 (top) The Last Record Store | Design Firm: GQ, New York | Design Director: Fred Woodward | Designer: Drue Wagner | Client: GQ

97 (bottom) Christian Bale | Design Firm: GQ, New York | Design Director: Fred Woodward | Designer: Anton Ioukhnovets | Client: GQ

98 (top) Quentin Tarantino | Design Firm: GQ, New York | Design Director: Fred Woodward | Designer: Delgis Canahuate | Client: GQ

98 (bottom) The Believer | Design Firm: GQ, New York | Design Director: Fred Woodward | Designer: Thomas Alberty | Client: GQ

99 (top) Zach Galafianakis | Design Firm: GQ, New York | Design Director: Fred Woodward | Designer: Chelsea Cardinal | Client: GQ

99 (bottom) Oh Betty! | Design Firm: GQ, New York | Design Director: Fred Woodward | Designer: Thomas Alberty | Client: GQ

100 noise24cover | Design Firm: Nuts About Design, Sydney | Art Director: Jason Smith | Assistant Editor: Shannon Smith | Creative Director, Editor: Mark Stapleton | Hair: Rodney Groves | Makeup: Walter Obal | Model: Ida | Photographer: Sarah Silver | Post-Production Manager, Production: Martine Wilson | Stylist: Christopher Campbell | Client: Highlights Publications

101 Metal #16 | Design Firm: Metal, Barcelona | Model: Sheila Márquez | Photographer: Xevi Muntané | Stylist: Ángela Esteban Librero | Client: Metal

102, 103 Muse Number 19, Fall 2009 | Design Firm: Lloyd & Company Advertising, Inc., New York | Art Director: Jason Evans, Martin Sandberg | Creative Director: Douglas Lloyd | Client: Muse Magazine

104 Directory 12 | Design Firm: SVIDesign, London | Creative Director: Sasha Vidakovic | Designers: Sarah Bates, Kat Egerer | Client: Direct New Ideas

Description: Directory is a quarterly magazine showcasing the best direct mail campaigns from around the world.

105 HOG Magazine | Design Firm: GS Design, Milwaukee | Art Directors: Paul Bartlett, Mark Brautigam | Project Manager: Alison Ban | Writer: Mike Zimmerman | Client: Harley-Davidson Motor Company

106, 107 NEWWORK Magazine Issue 4 | Design Firm: Studio NEWWORK, New York | Creative Director, Designer: Studio NEWWORK | Editor: Kate Quarfordt | Client: Studio NEWWORK

Description: NEWWORK Magazine is a large-format arts publication for connoisseur of fresh ideas. Designed and published biannually by Studio NEWWORK, each issue features new work from a wide range of artists and creators in the worlds of fine art, design, high fashion, culture, and politics. From art contributors to business leaders, design students to curators, NEWWORK's contributors are united in their passion to push the boundaries of their disciplines. Among the magazine's special features are bold, custom-designed typefaces and a twist on the traditional newspaper format, offering a stimulating juxtaposition of striking design and everyday simplicity. Since pages can be separated, each layout can be hung on the wall as an individual art piece. The fourth issue of NEWWORK Magazine finds a wide range of artists and designers harnessing the power of contrast in its various forms to bring dimension, meaning and mystery to their work. Witness the juicy juxtaposition of graphic and narrative elements in the iconic imagery of photographer Albert Watson. Observe the synergy of classic Swiss restraint and unbridled post-modern play in the typographic design of Wolfgang Weingart, and the kinetic interplay of geometric and organic forms in the poster design of Bruno Monguzzi. From the one-two punch of high contrast black-and-white forms in the photography of Julian Abram Wainwright and the drawings of Robert Longo, to the poetic tension between two and three dimensions in Werner Jeker's enigmatic collages, this issue profiles artists who use dynamic dualisms to yield complex and elegant visual solutions.

108 SOHI Magazine | Design Firm: Maud, Surry Hills | Art Directors: Sarah King, David Park, Rebecca Wolkenstein | Creative Director: Hampus Jageland | Photographer: Julian Wolkenstein | Print Producer: IMMIJ | Client: SOHI

Description: Maud created the corporate branding and art direction for SoHi; a new contemporary lifestyle magazine and website showcasing the Southern Highlands creative art and fashion scene. We continue to work with SoHi acting as brand guardian across all design content. We wanted to create a magazine which you'd want to keep on your coffee table for people to pick up or even pass on to a friend (Maud also designed a pass-it-on icon which has been used over the branding). Therefore, the main stories are designed to make the reader actually sit down and read rather than just quickly flick through it. As the stories are the main communication in the magazine, we wanted to put focus on its content. As the magazine would be a way of collecting all the most creative and interesting people in the Southern Highlands, we created a symbol to communicate this. It's designed to be perceived as a mix of a leaf, and the structure a leaf is built upon, and a diamond—a Southern Highlands diamond—which the magazine is trying to be perceived as. Just as a diamond is reflecting what's surrounding it, SOHI is too. The whole project was initially intended to be more blog focused, but since the SOHI crew, as well as the few lucky people getting their hands on an issue, loved it

so much, the SOHI crew continued to focus on the printed version.

109 (top) Brunswick Review | Design Firm: JohnstonWorks, London | Creative Director: Kirsten Johnston | Designers: Svetlana Andrienko, Remy Jauffret, Stuart Simpson | Editor: Timothy Dickson | Project Manager: Jo Piatek-Stewart | Client: Brunswick Group LLP

Description: Brunswick Review is a journal produced twice per year which incorporates topical and relevant issues surrounding corporate communications and corporate reputation. Written primarily by the Partners of the Brunswick Group, the publication aims to demonstrate Brunswick's breadth of expertise and is designed to for a global corporate audience. Brunswick Review has a print run of 28,000 copies and is distributed to 11 countries worldwide.

109 (middle) Dear Dave, Issue 6 | Design Firm: Visual Arts Press, Ltd., New York | Art Director, Designer: Michael J. Walsh | Creative Director: Anthony P. Rhodes | Client: School of Visual Arts

109 (bottom) Prefix Photo 20 | Design Firm: Underline Studio, Toronto | Creative Directors: Claire Dawson, Fidel Peña | Designer: Emily Tu | Client: Prefix Institute of Contemporary Art

Description: Prefix Photo is a magazine that presents contemporary Canadian photography in an international context. Characterized by innovative design and outstanding production values, it features photography portfolios and critical essays.

110, 111 PLATINUM Lush Winter 2009 | Design Firm: Lush Fashion & Art Magazine, Toronto | Art Director, Designer, Typographer: Paul Sych | Fashion Director: Serge Kerbel | Photographer: Lara Jade | Client: Lush Fashion & Art Magazine

112 abcDesign Magazine | Design Firm: Infolio, Curitiba | Art Director: Ericson Straub | Designer: Infolio (in house team) | Client: Infolio - abcDesign

Description: abcDesign magazine is a Brazilian publication that has been around since 2001. Printed magazines specialized in design are rare here. abcDesign is a one of a kind magazine in the country because it publishes in depth articles about both product and graphic design, dealing with not only what motivates and inspires designers, but also with the context of this fast growing professional field. The three issues sent to the Design Annual represent each one a different visual "phase" of the magazine.

Issue number 16 of 2006 represents basically abcDesign visual identity since its first issue. Due to a lack of financial resources, very few photographs were used, with the layout depending basically on balancing text, font, color and space. Issue number 22 of 2007 features on the cover a poster by German designer Pierre Mendell, and it represents the magazines second visual identity phase. Trying to move away from the previous stiff, square, bauhaus style, we started to use more organic forms, brighter colors, background images, patterns and illustration.

That went great for a while, but starting at 29th edition we added 16 more pages to the publication, which was a big achievement for us.

We decided to look back at our first visual style and realized that it was time to dose both our personalities: an immense admiration for the Swiss and German style with a contemporary visual language, which is what we are trying to achieve now.

113 design mind: The Substance of Things Not Seen | Design Firm: frog design, San Francisco | Editor: Sam Martin | Senior Designer: Jacob Zukerman | Client: frog design

Educational

114, 115 IDWRK 08 09 | Design Firm: cottage industries, Los Angeles | Designers: Erin Hauber, Davey Whitcraft | Client: University of Southern California School of Architecture

Description: IDWRK 08 09 is the inaugural publication showcasing student work from the USC School of Architecture. The school has distributed the book to current and prospective students, and will sell it in bookstores.

116 SVA Undergraduate Catalog 2010-11 | Design Firm: Visual Arts Press, Ltd., New York | Art Director: Michael J. Walsh | Creative Director: Anthony P. Rhodes | Designers: Suck Zoo Han, Brian E. Smith, E. Patrick Tobin | Client: School of Visual Arts

Description: The objective of the School of Visual Arts' undergraduate catalog, Proof, is to show prospective students why SVA is the preeminent training ground for the next generations of artists. We want to prove that SVA, located in NYC, is the best art school to attend. Our solution to that goal is to present visual and factual evidence, first by giving dozens of facts about NYC, SVA and its students, and then by presenting literally hundreds of examples of student work throughout the book.

117 MIT PLAN 73 | Design Firm: Philographica, Brookline | Art Director: David Horton | Designer: Amy LeBow | Photographer: Various | Writer: Scott Campbell | Client: MIT School of Architecture + Planning

Description: For nearly a decade, MIT's School of Architecture + Planning has relied on Philographica as a trusted advisor on marketing communications strategy. We produced the School's brand identity, designed its website, and created cost-effective design templates for its quarterly alumni publications. MIT SAP approached Philographica with the request that the publication strike a balance between heady written pieces and dynamic visual content. Multiple foldout stories, varying in length and topic, combine into a self-mailer, a format that significantly reduces mailing costs.

118, 119 601 Artbook Project 2009 - Catalog | Design Firm: 601bisang, Seoul | Art Director, Creative Director: Kum-jun Park | Designers: Kum-jun Park, Na-won You | Editor: So-youn Lee, Ji-sun Song | Executive Director: Jong-in Jung | Illustrator: Soo-hwan Kim | Photographer: Ok-hee Cho | Client: 601bisang

Description: Pictorial Record of 601 Art Book Project (2009). In the world of balance and harmony, contents make forms and forms improve contents.

This pictorial record for the 7th annual 601 Art Book Project gets viewers thinking about the concept of chiasm, an organic process whereby a fusion and exchange of materials takes place between nature, humans, raw materials and human spirit.
The 26 lines, which symbolize the 26 award-winning artists, were combined to form the letters "B" and "H" on the front and back covers of the pictorial record. These letters represent the exhibition concepts of balance and harmony. Every page of these award-winning art books was designed so that they had an individual character related to the overall theme of the book. Each page with an illustration that shows an award-winning artist's work as an image is an important tool to reveal that particular artist's identity. It also adds an emotional element to the pictorial record.
Twenty-six symbolic lines, which run from the cover to the inside of the pictorial record, were applied to the exhibition poster. They were also applied three-dimensionally to the exhibition hall and to all of the promotional activities for the event.

120, 121 View Book | Design Firm: Studio Hinrichs, San Francisco | Creative Director: Kit Hinrichs | Printer: Blanchette Press | Project Manager: Adi Wise | Senior Designer: Takayo Muroga | Strategy Director: Peterson Skolnick & Dodge | Writer: Betsy Brown | Client: Embry-Riddle Aeronautical University

Description: Embry-Riddle Aeronautical University is recognized and respected worldwide as a center of cutting edge instruction and education for tomorrow's aviation and aerospace leaders. Embry-Riddle engaged Studio Hinrichs to design a View Book for prospective students that demonstrates the quality of education, facilities and faculty available at this institution. For the student and parent, well-designed and appropriate materials can be a vital factor in determining a choice of school. For the staff, they generate pride and a sense of mission in the institution. For the University, they can become a strong foundation to lead it into the future.

Environmental

122, 123 Jay Jays Robina Store Design | Design Firm: Saatchi Design Worldwide, Auckland | Creative Director: Derek Lockwood | Design Director: Blake Enting | Designers: George Kivell, Kane McPherson | Managing Director: Mike Ensor (Three Sixty Limited) | Project Manager: Jessica Taylor | Client: The Just Group

Description: Jay Jays Robina Store Concept: Jay Jays is a low-price clothing retailer targeting 16-23 year olds. Their customers are incredibly diverse—Emos Goths, Surfies, Street kids, Preppies, Hipsters and more. For youth, freedom of self-expression comes when they are "out" away from the controls of parents and authority. The store uses the "street" as a metaphor for the place where youth can be "out", experimenting with their style. It provides an irreverent, engaging environment that celebrates diversity.

124 Corporate Design for the Dornier Museum Friedrichshafen | Design Firm: häfelinger+wagner design, Munich | Creative Director: Frank Wagner | Client: CODO Projektbüro GmbH

Description: Dornier decisively influenced the history of air travel with a pioneering spirit and technical innovations. The fascination of flying and—through the perspective of the pictography—the sight of an aeroplane flying in the sky are the focus of the corporate design of the Aerospace Museum. It stands as inspirational, almost poetic symbol and homage to the pioneering spirit, for the dream of flying. The film version of the logo depicts the dynamic appearance of a clouded sky from the point of view of an aeroplane.

125 Liquid Bar | Design Firm: Lorenc+Yoo Design, Roswell | Project Manager: Matt Walker | Client: Northern Quest Casino & Resort

Description: We designed the primary identification signage for the liquid bar at the new expansion to the Northern Quest Casino in Spokane, Washington. We designed the letterforms and specified all materials and fabrication. The sign is internally illuminated with a series of led lights and the letterforms are made of color backed acrylic panels.

126, 127 LAF Headquarters Environmental Graphics | Design Firm: fd2s, Austin | Creative Director: Curtis Roberts | Designer: Jordan Kepsel | Project Manager: Leslie Wolke | Client: The Lance Armstrong Foundation

Description: Founded in 1997 by cancer survivor and champion cyclist Lance Armstrong, the Lance Armstrong Foundation (LAF) has raised more than $260 million for the fight against cancer. The organization's new headquarters facility, a renovation of the 30,000-square-foot Gulf Paper warehouse in East Austin, houses foundation staff and also supports the survivorship mission by providing space for programs and activities.
fd2s created a graphics program for the headquarters that turns the building's public spaces into a venue for conveying the mission, history, and achievements of the LAF and its many constituent groups, while also providing opportunities to recognize LAF donors. A recurring motif of the program is a yellow band with recessed or cut out type, which is a tribute the foundation's most recognized symbol, the yellow wristbands that have raised tens of millions of dollars, one dollar at a time.
The building is on track to achieve Gold LEED certification, and fd2s contributed to this effort by working with the signage fabricator to use surplus materials from the fabricator's shop wherever possible.

128, 129 Microsoft Visitor Center Experience Design | Design Firm: Hornall Anderson, Seattle | Account Director: Ricki Pasinelli | Associate Creative Director: SkB Architects | Creative Directors: Mark Popich, SkB Architects | Designers: Rachel Blakley, Tony DeVincenzi, Ethan Keller, Don Kenoyer, Jessica Lennard, Drew Pickard, Yumiko Suda, Andrew Well, Nathan Young | Project Managers: Danial Crookston, Dana Kruse, Chris Monberg, Kevin Roth, Halli Thiel | Strategy Director: Sunita Richardson | Web Developers: Matt Frickelton, Gordon Mueller, Corey Paganucci | Client: Microsoft Corporation

Description: By weaving together Microsoft's products, services and vision into a rich experience, Hornall Anderson helped bring the multi-faceted brand to life in a more publicly accessible way. Our goal was to transform the new, 10,000 square-foot Visitor Center into a holistic experience that connects visitors with Microsoft's brand through tangible and entertaining interactions. By first authoring the desired customer experience story and then leveraging a mix of the physical and virtual, we created a series of analogue, interactive, and digital media installations that connect people with the life-enriching capabilities of Microsoft technology. The result is a highly branded space that encourages curiosity, interaction and helps Microsoft present itself as a true multi-faceted innovator.

130, 131 Microsoft B111 Candidate Lobby Experience Design | Design Firm: Hornall Anderson, Seattle | Account Director: Ricki Pasinelli | Associate Creative Director: ZGF Architects | Creative Director: Larry Anderson | Designers: Rachel Blakley, Holly Craven, Adrien Lo, Nivi Ramesh, Leo Raymundo, Andrew Well, Nathan Young | Print Producers: Paula Cox, Julie Valdez, Jeff Wolff | Project Manager: Halli Thiel | Strategy Director: Lee Ann Johnson | Web Developers: Gordon Mueller, Corey Paganucci | Client: Microsoft Corporation

Description: Interpreting a personality in a 3-dimensional space. This was the challenge when we were charged with branding the new Microsoft Candidate Lobby in partnership with ZGF Architects. The objective was to create a memorable space that clearly communicates the Microsoft recruitment brand goals, while affirming that it is a dynamic and smart place to work. Our team strategically centered first on defining the Microsoft Recruitment core values, and then on how they are manifested into a physical space. The focus was to provide candidates visiting the campus with a portrait of what Microsoft has to offer and the smart, innovative people who work for the cutting-edge technology company. Candidates are also invited to share their own stories and concurrently learn about Microsoft employee stories in an interactive environment. Upon entering, visitors experience how a 3-dimensional space becomes alive and the walls become portraits of possibilities, all through three areas of engagement: My Story, Your Story and Our Story. The reaction at Microsoft has been overwhelming; it's like nothing they've ever had before.
"Our Story" is comprised of the Imagine wall, the last in an interactive analog art display. The wall holds a series of plex panels that show photos and quotes from current employees spelling the word Imagine. Candidates are invited to fill out a card asking them to say in a few words how they imagine their role at Microsoft, and then apply it to the display.
The "Your Story" Focal wall is an interactive dimensional art wall connected to two touch screens that prompt the applicant to share some of their interests, goals and reasons for applying at Microsoft. All these create an electronic profile, which is digitized and displayed as a stylized representation on a series of five screens that are connected to create a personalized mosaic. These images rotate throughout the day making the candidate the hero for the day.

132, 133 Willis Tower Skydeck Queuing Interactive Experience | Design Firm: Hornall Anderson, Seattle | Account Director: Erin Crosier | Creative Directors: Ashley Arhart, Jamie Monberg, Andrew Wicklund | Designers: Larry Anderson, Rachel Blakley, Elmer dela Cruz, Tony DeVincenzi, Chris Freed, Jon Graeff, Kalani Gregoire, Jay Hilburn, Oliver Hutton, Don Kenoyer, Joseph King, Hans Krebs, Jessica Lennard, Adrien Lo, Drew Pickard, Nivi Ramesh, Samuel Stubblefield, Andrew Well | General Director: Soraya Gallego | Illustrators: Greg Arhart, Jay Hilburn | Print Producers: Paula Cox, Judy Dixon, Peg Johnson, Jonas Land, Julie Valdez, Jeff Wolff | Project Managers: Dana Kruse, Zak Menkel, Chris Monberg, Kevin Roth, Halli Thiel | Web Developers: Matt Frickelton, Gordon Mueller | Writers: Bill Hollister, Ben Steele | Client: Willis Tower

Description: Seeking to bridge its iconic legacy with its state-of-the-art vision of the future, Skydeck Chicago—located in the Willis Tower (formerly the Sears Tower)—tasked us with creating an end-to-end immersive Skydeck queuing experience to celebrate this world-renowned tourist destination and demonstrate real connections to the legacy and future of the Tower, while achieving key business goals of increasing visitor traffic to more than one million and driving additional revenue per guest.
The Skydeck queue is comprised of three major experiences that blend environmental graphics, digital interaction and sculptural elements designed to engage visitors and encourage visual and tactile interaction. The scope of the overall project includes the Skydeck identity redesign, visitor queuing experience, movie and elevator ride, with plans to grow the experience design to a more holistic extension.
The experience emphasizes creating memories—something the visitor will never forget, whether virtually looking down over local landmarks from 103 stories high, to learning various factoids about the Tower and the city's cultural life through a mix of digital touch screens, wall graphics and a movie compilation of the Tower's history. It paces visitors on a journey at every level from point of entry to exit, utilizing content that leverages iconic moments in the Tower and Chicago culture. The experience encompasses three different themed rooms: the Tower Room, Iconic Chicago Room and Skyscrapers—the latter filled with "fun with height" comparisons.

134, 135 PLATINUM Madison Square Garden Presentation Center Interactive Experience | Design Firm: Hornall Anderson, Seattle | Account Director: Erin Crosier | Associate Creative Director: TPG Architects | Creative Directors: Ashley Arhart, Jamie Monberg | Designers: Belinda Bowling,

Tony DeVincenzi, Jon Graeff, Owen Irianto, Leo Raymundo, John Rousseau, Hayden Schoen, Samuel Stubblefield, Andrew Well, Nathan Young | Illustrator: Greg Arhart, Tom Price | Photographer: Alec Zaballero | Print Producers: Paula Cox, Judy Dixon, Julie Valdez, Jeff Wolff | Project Managers: Zak Menkel, Chris Monberg, Kevin Roth, Halli Thiel | Strategy Director: Lee Ann Johnson | Web Developers: Matt Frickelton, Trevor Hartman, Gordon Mueller, Corey Paganucci | Writer: Joe Moore | Client: Madison Square Garden

Description: Virtualizing the view. When Madison Square Garden tapped us to design their Presentation Center interactive experience, it was to reposition the brand essence of the legendary landmark. The objective was to create a Presentation Center comprised of cutting edge technology and design to communicate the upgraded suite and partnership offering and demonstrate the vision of Madison Square Garden's future in a tangible way. More than the typical marketing center, the new MSG Presentation Center creates an immersive guest experience. Through a blend of physical and digital experiential design, we created a variety of simulated views of the arena from different vantage points. The space unfolds in a theatrical and dramatic unveiling of ambient lighting and surrounds people with a story that comes alive through timed and paced emotional content. It evokes memories and excitement not unlike being at an actual evening at the Garden. The overall results excite each visitor with the unique Garden experience and all that it has to offer through a mix of traditional and digital interactions and content that expresses the rich history of the Garden.

Exhibits

136, 137 The Storyteller's Art, Exhibition | Design Firm: Studio Hinrichs, San Francisco | Creative Director: Kit Hinrichs | Designer: Gloria Hiek, An Luc | Project Manager: Adi Wise | Writer: Delphine Hirasuna | Client: Art Center College of Design

Description: The Storyteller's Art, a forty-year retrospective of Kit Hinrichs's design work, presents more than 200 pieces of his work. In this exhibition poster, the designer's portrait is illustrated with type, and his familiar white beard emerges from biographical copy. The show considers Hinrichs's designs—his choice of imagery, color, typeface and printing technique—as vehicles for storytelling. "What characterizes his work—whether it's a corporate identity, museum exhibition, magazine or book—is a compelling storyline that communicates what the entity is all about in a manner that is evocative and memorable," says Library Gallery Director Phillip Hitchcock. "Kit relies on storytelling devices—pacing, narrative voice, irony, surprise, humor, pathos—to engage audiences emotionally and draw them into the story in thought-provoking and memorable ways."

138, 139 Teknion Exhibit | Design Firm: Vanderbyl Design, San Francisco | Art Director, Creative Director: Michael Vanderbyl | Designers: Peter Fishel, David Hard, Michael Vanderbyl | Client: Teknion Furniture Systems

Description: Teknion's commitment to sustainable business practices encompasses the design, development and manufacture of all its products. These same principles inform our design choices for the new 2009 IIDEX exhibit. To address the exhibit's modest size (1200 square feet), the IIDEX booth was constructed with a 16' high surround that is suspended off the floor 1"-6". This "floating" wall creates an appropriate enclosure that directs the visitor's attention to the product, while also creating an illusion of spaciousness as the floor extends visually well past the wall-defined space.

Keeping responsible use of materials in mind, exhibit walls are fabricated of fully recyclable aluminum and spandex and carpeting has been reused from last year's IIDEX booth. The nature-inspired graphics printed on the spandex interior offer vivid symbols of Teknion's commitment to the natural environment. As a showcase for Teknion's latest products, the exhibit highlights ACER, a new line developed in partnership with ACER Design A/S of Bogense, Denmark. The first new offerings include a collaborative lounge seating system and mobile worktables, which are used in the booth to create an inviting space for conversation about Teknion's WorkplaceOne concept. To facilitate dialogue further, two large video screens offer a multimedia presentation of the ideas that animate WorkplaceOne. Beyond the multimedia display, laptop computers placed on the ACER product illustrate its functionality and also allow visitors to view a visual fly-through of the WorkplaceOne concept.

Like Teknion's thoughtfully designed products, and the new WorkplaceOne concept, the 2009 IIDEX exhibit stresses the intelligent use of resources—space, light and materials—to sustain a healthy, productive workplace.

140 Sikorsky Exhibit | Design Firm: McMillan Group, Westport | Account Director: Tara Dziurman | Creative Strategist: Elaine Cohen | Designers: Charlie McMillan, Nancy McMillan | Managing Director: Alph Leydon | Photographer: Michel Guyon-Line 8 Photography | Project Managers: Rob Harper, Anne Trompeter | Client: Sikorsky

Description: The project was to design an exhibit for Sikorsky, a leader in helicopter design and manufacturing. The 80'x180' by 20' high exhibit was for the largest industry show, Heli-Expo in Anaheim Convention Center and premiered on February 22, 2009. The purpose was to embody a unique new world class exhibit brand architecture that communicated and expressed the changes in the organization, reinforcing customer service and unifying the entire company. The goal was to create an environment that was conducive to business, client-focused, and exemplified Sikorsky as a global industry leader. The client required that the exhibit have a high end product "showroom" to showcase helicopters, services and technological advancements. Functionally the exhibit was developed into two distinct sections: an open,

more "public" showcase display of aircraft and live shows with large scale media support for all attendees and a more private executive boardroom level meeting room structure. The design of the exhibit, and specifically the two story structures, expressed the energy of rotary winged flight as two off set curved and cantilevered conference room structures

141 Plug-and-play bank | Design Firm: VBAT, Amsterdam | Account Director: Koen Koster | Creative Directors: Andy Palmer-Smith, Stefan Pangratz | Designers: Maarten van Disseldorp, Juliet Wong | Senior Designers: Jim Taylor, Meriel Verheul | Strategy Director: Eugene Bay | Client: SNS Bank

Description: How to cater for the changing consumer needs of long-term client, SNS Bank—a 24/7 online access with the reassurance of personal advice. Respecting the belief that physical bank shops play a key role in building relationships and driving sales, VBAT utilised the impact of customer-focused retail principles to create a fresh colourful space that embraces the accessibility and convenience of on-line banking. The minimised floor space comprises six colour-coded POP units providing take-me-home customer driven information via touchscreens technology and tangible product cards. A physical space with an on-the-go (online) interface—a new generation of retail bank.

142, 143 IIDEX Exhibit | Design Firm: Vanderbyl Design, San Francisco | Art Director, Creative Director: Michael Vanderbyl | Designers: Peter Fishel, David Hard, Michael Vanderbyl | Client: Teknion Furniture Systems

Description: Teknion's goal for the exhibit was to bring focused attention to Teknion's leadership in sustainable development. As part of Teknion's responsibility to sustainability every aspect of the exhibit was designed with this in mind. Materials include MDF and plywood both of which are 100% FSC certified, the metals have a high recycled content, the finishes are water-based and the booth was manufactured locally. At the end of the show, the trees were donated to the Orphan Spaces—a Toronto program in partnership with the Design Exchange—and the booth components stored for future use. The furniture and the new Optos glass wall system are re-locatable and are Greenguard and ECO Logo certified. In addition to the physical aspects of the exhibit, each tree pedestal describes a step Teknion has taken in their commitment to sustainability. As part of the exhibit concept, Teknion LEED accredited professionals shared their insights and knowledge with visitors so that together we all can make a difference.

144, 145 United States Capitol Visitor Center | Design Firm: Ralph Appelbaum Associates Inc, New York | Creative Strategists: Jessica Holbrook, Evelyn Reilly, Sarah van Haastert, Deborah Wolff | Design Director: Melanie Ide, Marianne Schuit | Designers: John Boyer, James Cathcart, Josh Hartley, Helene Kenny, Luka Kito, Ryan Koslowski, Christiaan Kuypers, John Locascio, Christopher Miceli, Lisa Paruch, Michelle Reeb, George Robertson, Scott Shepard, Tim Ventimiglia | Editors: Niki Amadur, Sylvia Juran | Executive Director: Ralph Appelbaum | Client: Architect of the Capitol

Description: This new underground expansion at the United States Capitol Visitor Center in Washington, D.C., provides orientation, interpretive experiences and visitor amenities to more than four million people each year. Located on the lower level of the Capitol Visitor Center, the exhibit hall showcases documents, artifacts, images and video that tell the history of the United States Congress and the U.S. Capitol building. Upon entering the exhibition, visitors encounter an eleven-foot-tall model of the Capitol dome and a changing display of National Archive treasures, which tell the story of our national aspirations. From there, visitors can examine the history of Congress and the United States Constitution through rare documents and artifacts. Interactive displays provide more in depth information, while two theaters offer an interactive and live window into the daily workings for Congress today.

The inspirational 16,500-square-foot exhibit is in keeping with the dignity and beauty of the Capitol. The exhibit tells the story of American representative government and the building that houses it. A dramatic 200-foot-long display features rare documents that are touchstones of our democracy, as well as artifacts that tell the history of Congress and the Capitol. Two theater-like spaces offer a virtual experience of being in the galleries of the House and Senate, and "go live" when Congress is in session. Interactive exhibits explore the building's architecture, art, and decorative arts, and special programs aim to inspire young people to participate in the democratic process. The design focused on creating a space with an open, simple flow that seamlessly highlights the rich history of the Capitol building and Congress. The design allows for the display of rare, precious artifacts and documents in addition to computer and video interactives that provide in depth and current information.

Illustration

146 Literary Arts: Julia de Burgos | Art Director: Howard E. Paine | Artist: Jody Hewgill | Client: United States Postal Service

147 PLATINUM Cowboys of the Silver Screen | Art Director: Carl T. Herrman | Artist: Robert Rodriguez | Client: United States Postal Service

148 Permanent Line | Design Firm: Peter Kraemer, Düsseldorf | Illustrator: Peter Kraemer | Client: Peter Kraemer

Description: Illustration of a barbed wire, made of yellow pencils, for self promotion.

149 Bixby Bridge | Art Director: Carl T. Herrman | Artist: Dan Cosgrove | Client: United States Postal Service

Credits&Comments

150 Castrol Ultimax Product Launch | Design Firm: oakwood media group, Bristol | Account Director: Rebecca Petrie | Art Director: Jess Britton | Creative Director: Neil Sims | Illustrator: Jim Meston | Client: Castrol Offshore

Description: Castrol Offshore launched a range of high performance lubrication solutions with a new visualisation of "The Liquid Engineer" inspired from the long standing master brand sign of, "It's more than just oil, it's Liquid Engineering." Previewed at the Global Offshore Technology Conference in Houston, Texas, the world's largest Energy and Power trade event, the Castrol Ultimax range delivers maximum reliability under the most arduous of conditions. Strategic Offer Manager Phil Michaelis states, "The Liquid Engineer is not a single entity, but the embodiment of a core Castrol Offshore value, The Strength Within. The character is portrayed as a global lubrication specialist exuding confidence, operational security and above all intelligent protection." oakwood media group created and developed the overarching look and feel for the character who appears on the Exhibition stand, a range of online materials, e-books and launch video.

151 Pencil Bomb | Design Firm: Peter Kraemer, Düsseldorf | Illustrator: Peter Kraemer | Client: Peter Kraemer

Description: Illustration of a time bomb made of red pencils for a greeting card.

152 Caution | Design Firm: Goodby, Silverstein & Partners, San Francisco | Account Director: Ladd Martin | Art Director: Ryan Meis | Associate Creative Directors: Brian Gunderson, John Park | Executive Creative Director: Steve Simpson | Photographer: Zachary Scott | Print Producer: Hillary Talltree | Client: Hewlett Packard

Description: The brief for the ads was simple and, unusual for advertising, based on truth: Original HP Inks are in fact far more reliable than the refills people often buy. That said, the product itself is mundane. To give our message some heat, we found inspiration in the energy and directness of early 20th century PSA posters. All the art work was built practically, which we thought helped update the universe these things usually live in.

153 (top) Sprint Nextel Business Campaign 1 | Design Firm: Goodby, Silverstein & Partners, San Francisco | Art Director: Sheldon Melvin | Creative Director: Mark Dunn, Mike Mazza | Illustrator: Superfad | Print Producer: Alisa Latvala | Writer: Sha Nguyen | Client: Sprint

Description: We spoke directly to people working in Federal Government, Local Government and Public Safety by creating startling situations that required closer attention, yet somehow spoke to concerns that were all to common to our targets.

153 (bottom), **154** Sprint Nextel Business Campaign 2 | Design Firm: Goodby, Silverstein & Partners, San Francisco | Art Directors: Andy Babbitz, Sheldon Melvin | Creative Directors: Mark Dunn, Mike Mazza | Illustrator: Superfad | Print Producer: Alisa Latvala | Writers: Thomas Kemeny, Sha Nguyen | Client: Sprint

Description: We spoke directly to people working in local Government, Manufacturing and Transportation by creating startling situations that required closer attention, yet somehow spoke to concerns that were all to common to our targets.

Interactive

155 www.callawaygolf.com/hititpure | Design Firm: Hello Design, Culver City | Account Director: Scott Arenstein | Creative Directors: David Lai, Hiro Niwa | Design Director: Sung Hean Baik | Designers: Hajime Himeno, Christine Yu | Project Manager: Barry Chiang | Web Developer: Steven Sacks | Client: Callaway Golf

Description: There is no better feeling in golf than hitting a pure shot, and with Callaway Golf's latest Fusion drivers—the FT-iQ and the FT-9—players will be able to hit more pure shots more often. We created an online game for Callaway Golf that provides players with an engaging way to experience their two new drivers. Take the drivers out for a test drive on either the golf course or the driving range. Players get 10 shots to try to drive the ball as far as they can to achieve the top score. Hitting a Pure Shot reveals a special reward and there are hidden bonuses and secret codes that can be entered during game play to enable power-ups. Players can find these codes throughout CallawayGolf.com which encourages users to explore the site and learn more about the drivers in more detail. Go ahead, hit it pure.

156 Taking Root: The Joyce Foundation 2008 | Design Firm: Kym Abrams Design, Chicago | Creative Director: Kym Abrams | Designer: Deborah Sherwin | Photographers: Leland Bobbe, Augustus Butera, Carroll & Carroll, Randy Faris/Corbis, FK Photo/Corbis, Getty Images, Joan Marcus, Charlie Simokaitis | Print Producer: Unique Active | Web Developer: Thirdwave, LLC | Writer: Emily Blum | Client: The Joyce Foundation

Description: The print piece acts as a teaser for the full report online: www.joycefdn.org/ar. 2008 was a momentous year for the Joyce Foundation. After decades-long investments of effort and resources, the foundation saw key achievements come to fruition across its various initiatives. The report highlights those successes and the people across the nation enriched by the work.

157 www.sony.com/altus | Design Firm: Hello Design, Culver City | Account Director: George Lee | Creative Directors: David Lai, Hiro Niwa | Design Director: Sung Hean Baik | Designers: Hajime Himeno, Christine Yu | Project Manager: Barry Chiang | Web Developer: Steven Sacks | Client: Sony

Description: Sony's launch of the Altus wireless multi-room music system introduces a new way to enjoy music from a PC, iPod, or an existing stereo across multiple rooms. Our team concepted, directed, and produced an integrated campaign that includes a video-driven microsite, posters at the point-of-sale, and a series of live action videos for interactive retail kiosks for Best Buy and Sony Style. The microsite showcases a series of rooms in a house where a couple uses Altus products to listen to and control their music from room to room. Users can find detailed product features by selecting embedded hot spots. Configuring Altus for your home is easily done by choosing a music source and number of rooms, with the option of buying directly from Sony Style with a single click. "Music Everywhere, Wires Nowhere."

158 Ashburton Animations | Design Firm: Arthur Steen Horne Adamson, Cheltenham | Art Director: Marksteen Adamson | Design Director: Scott McGuffie | Designers: Chris Greenwood, Joe Hole, Asli Kalinoglu, Zoe Lester | Client: Ashburton

Description: In the Autumn of 2007 ASHA was appointed to revitalise the Ashburton brand. Ashburton is an investment management company headquartered in Jersey and with offices around the world. It delivers a range of products to intermediaries, institutional investors and private clients.
Their distinctive investment philosophy is built on an active and unconstrained approach that allows the investment professionals freedom of thought and capacity for bold and insightful action. This means that although Ashburton uses the same component parts as any other investment house, they are able to create unique funds. We therefore developed an illustration style that takes everyday office objects, but combines them in interesting ways to create beautiful and unusual illustrations. An animal illustration appropriate to each fund was created. Animations were created to communicate the "normalness" of the component parts of the illustrations, but at the same time catch the eye, and raise awareness of the particular fund.

159 The Meyer May House Next 100 presented by Steelcase Inc. | Design Firm: Genesis, Inc., Denver | Art Directors: Janelle Key, Mario Rini | Creative Director: Matt Ward | Executive Creative Strategist: Georgia Everse | Web Developer: Josh Pangell | Writer: Eileen Raphael | Client: Steelcase Inc

Invitations

160 2009 Tuna Party Invite: "Bare Bones" | Design Firm: Wallace Church, Inc., New York | Creative Director: Stan Church | Designers: Tiphaine Guillemet, Becca Reiter, Kim Young | Illustrator: Becca Reiter | Client: Wallace Church, Inc

Description: "Bare Bones" is all you'll find at the end of Wallace Church's annual tuna party, where we cook up delicious fresh tuna on the grill and celebrate with friends and clients. Our invitation this year features an elegant, laser-cut tuna suspended from a hook and line inside an acrylic presentation box, like a rare specimen. It is suspended over a small, four-fold invitation, neatly tucked into the bottom of the box. The invitation is printed black with our signature Wallace Church logo on the top panel. As each panel is unfolded the invitation reveals itself, opening finally on a subtle image of the tuna, printed shiny black on black.

161 SVA Theatre Opening Invitation | Design Firm: Milton Glaser Inc., New York | Designers: Milton Glaser, Sue Walsh | Photographer: Jim Brown | Printer: GHP Printing | Client: School of Visual Arts

162 HKDA Awards 09 Invitation Card | Design Firm: Eric Chan Design Co. Ltd., Causeway Bay | Art Director, Creative Director: Eric Chan | Designers: Eric Chan, Manson Chan | Client: Hong Kong Designers Association

Letterhead

163 DINAMO LETTERHEAD | Design Firm: Eduardo del Fraile, Murcia | Creative Director, Design Director: Eduardo del Fraile | Senior Designer: Andres Guerrero | Client: DINAMO

Description: The company focuses on providing advice vis-à-vis the collection of solar energy for the development of photovoltaic plants. The graphic proposal involved using the typography of the dynamo brand as a light collector to store energy during the day.

164 Sculpture Business Card | Design Firm: David Ferris Design, New York | Designer: David Ferris | Client: David Ferris

Description: I needed business cards for my work as a sculptor, and wanted a solution that would reflect the conceptual manner in which I approach my work. So I developed a business card that transforms into a "do-it-yourself" sculpture.

165 Actions speak louder than logos | Design Firm: thomas.matthews, London | Creative Directors: Tara Hanrahan, Sophie Thomas | Designer: Peter Clarkson | Print Producer: Calverts | Client: thomas.matthews

Description: We felt it was about time we piped up about our 12-year commitment to sustainable communications. We looked at what we do and how we do it, to define the values that shape our work, i.e. We believe in good* design. *appropriate, sustainable and beautiful. We pushed ourselves and our printer to the limit, to create a set of truly fabulous stationery, that is:
Appropriate – communicates our ethos through the messages and the medium
Sustainable – has been produced entirely from waste materials.
Beautiful – uses bold colours and tactile metallics to reveal inspiring and challenging statements.
Here's the story of how we did it:
Paper – We know that by switching to a post-consumer recycled stock we can save up to 70% of the embodied energy of a piece of print. But then we thought, what if we use paper that is already sitting in our printer's warehouse because of an over order? We riffled through their surplus stock and chose some suitable weights and finishes. We didn't stop there. We asked our printer to use it as "make-ready" (paper that preps the press on a number of jobs). Once it had finished this useful task, we saved it from being discarded.
Inks – Even with vegetable-based ones there's a story. They may be low in VOC's (Volatile Organic Chemicals) and less polluting, but there are some serious questions around soy crops causing rainforest deforestation to contend with. Every time a designer asks for a particular spot colour (even for

the smallest job) the printer mixes up a tin. That's a whole litre of ink when you may only require a spoonful. So instead of contributing to this global impact, we spent an afternoon peering into leftover pots (checking them for low barium and copper along the way) to arrive at our new brand palette. We checked the supplier's specification and asked some experts about the use of metallics and the effect of using big floods of colour on the de-inking process and they responded by telling us that our approach was great and would not detract from the overall recyclability of the finished article.

Imposition – Now we had our colours and materials, we could combine these with our knowledge of the press sheet space and start designing. It may seem a backward process starting with the restriction of leftovers and the production process—but it made perfect sense to us!

166 Identity Package | Design Firm: Toolbox Design, Vancouver | Designer: Peter Ladd | Client: Quick McMorran

Description: If you happen to be doing corporate branding and sponsorship work at some of the world's biggest sporting events, you don't get noticed by being anything but ultra creative and particularly brilliant. Quick McMorran needed an identity, website and stationary package that would reflect their way-outside-the-box thought process. So we came up with something that can be described as punchy, gallant, a little cheeky—even a bit mental. And of course, it fits them like a glove.

167 Day One Letterhead | Design Firm: 3 Advertising, Albuquerque | Account Director: Chris Moore | Creative Director: Sam Maclay | Design Director: Tim McGrath | Client: Day One LLC

Description: Letterhead package for Day One, a holding company for creative businesses.

Logos

168 (1ˢᵗ) FEED logo | Design Firm: Martin Williams | Chief Creative Officer: Tom Moudry | Creative Directors: Julie Kucinski, David Richardson | Designer: Gabe Gathmann | Client: MIMA

168 (3ʳᵈ) Gubbins Light and Power Company Logo | Design Firm: Ventress Design Group, Inc., Nashville | Designer: Tom Ventress | Client: Gubbins Light and Power Company

168 (4ᵗʰ) Saveurs D'ailleurs | Design Firm: Yonalee Design, Astoria | Art Director: Yona Lee | Designer: Jee-eun Lee | Client: Saveurs D'ailleurs

Description: Logo for a take-out restaurant in Switzerland serving dishes from different countries. "Saveurs d'ailleurs" literally means "tastes from elsewhere."

168 (5ᵗʰ) Su's ceramics logo | Design Firm: Haas Design, Edinburgh | Designer: Oliver Haas | Client: Susan Kemp Ceramics

Description: Logo for Susan Kemp Ceramics. Susan Kemp Ceramics is a small start-up business selling hand-thrown pottery from a Scottish studio and at local markets. Susan required a simple and versatile logo not only for use on stationery and promotional material but also to be stamped directly onto the ceramics and paper bags. The logo reflects that this craft business is all about Su's personality: It can be read as Su's craft (pottery), her name, and a caricature of her face.

168 (2ⁿᵈ), **169** Oakland Logo | Design Firm: Wall-to-Wall Studios, Pittsburgh | Creative Directors: James Nesbitt, Larkin Werner | Designer: Doug Dean | Client: Oakland Community Council

Description: Wall-to-Wall Studios developed the logo and branding for the community of Oakland via the Oakland Community Council, which represents the needs of residents and institutions. Oakland derived its name from the abundance of oak trees found in the community and is the third largest commerce center in Pennsylvania. The neighborhood re-branding initiative came from a desire to: identify boundaries, create a sense of place, of community, of welcome, and instill neighborhood pride.

170 Greyhound Logo | Design Firm: Butler, Shine, Stern & Partners, Sausalito | Design Director: Neal Zimmerman | Designer: Ajana Green | Executive Creative Directors: John Butler, Mike Shine | Client: Greyhound

171 (1ˢᵗ) Gallery 64 | Design Firm: Yonalee Design, Astoria | Art Director: Yona Lee | Designer: Jee-eun Lee | Client: Gallery 64

171 (2ⁿᵈ) Catalina Pizza logo | Design Firm: MacLaren McCann Calgary, Calgary | Art Director, Designer: Sean Mitchell | Creative Director: Mike Meadus | Client: Catalina Pizza

Description: Logo for a modern art gallery in Switzerland.

171 (3ʳᵈ) Honey | Design Firm: Texas State University, San Marcos | Art Director: Keo Pierron | Client: Honey

Description: A logo was developed for a gastro lounge in Minneapolis, MN. A gastro lounge is a new idea of a more sophisticated eating and drinking establishment where elegant small plates are served, and the drinks are more refined and stylish. The concept for the lounge's logo involves a bee and a wine glass.

171 (4ᵗʰ) Medicine in Motion Logo | Design Firm: 3 Advertising, Albuquerque | Account Director: Chris Moore | Creative Director: Sam Maclay | Design Director: Tim McGrath | Client: Medicine in Motion

Description: A mobile medicine clinic.

171 (5ᵗʰ) Culinary District | Design Firm: fabrizio design, New York | Designer: Steven Fabrizio | Client: Culinary District

Description: Culinary District—Place to shop and find huge selection of cooking utensils and food products for the serious chef, restaurant owner and the novice cook.

172 (1ˢᵗ) POLLOCK | Design Firm: POLLOCK, Calgary | Creative Director: Keli Pollock | Client: Keli Pollock

Description: Logo for POLLOCK creative services which provides art direction, design and writing services.

172 (2ⁿᵈ) Kuka | Design Firm: Yonalee Design, Astoria | Art Director: Yona Lee | Designer: Jee-eun Lee | Client: Kuka Escapes

Description: Logo for a luxury bed-and-breakfast chain by the Mediterranean. "Kuka" means "seagull" in Italian.

172 (3ʳᵈ) San Anselmo Public Library | Design Firm: Michael Schwab Studio, San Anselmo | Designer: Michael Schwab | Client: San Anselmo Public Library

172 (4ᵗʰ) Ihu Logo | Design Firm: Saatchi Design Worldwide, Auckland | Creative Director, Designer: Blake Enting | Client: Ihu

Description:

The Company – Ihu (meaning "to rest" in the language of the New Zealand Maori) is a luxury accommodation brand. It is specifically targeting potential overseas (rather than local) visitors that wish to experience a unique New Zealand getaway.

The Solution – The logo uses the godwit as a metaphor for travelers coming to New Zealand—the bird that makes the longest flight in the world from the northern hemisphere to New Zealand. There are three different lockups for the logo to allow for flexible application. In each, the godwit is resting after its flight, the tall text of the logo extended to mimic the poles of a wharf, the bird on top.

Ihu Brand Story – In late September as summer winds down to golden autumn, the eastern bar-tailed godwit takes flight from the coast of Alaska. For seven long days and nights it flies, following the arc of the earth far into the vast southern ocean, not resting until it comes finally to the distant island sanctuaries of Aotearoa, New Zealand. For 11,000 kilometres it journeys, the longest non-stop flight of any bird in the world. It comes seeking replenishment, a place to rest and the start of spring.

Man has always watched the skies. Searching for signs of providence, hearts yearning for what lies beyond the horizon. So it was before Polynesian voyagers set off to explore the Pacific, the flight of the godwit (or kuaka) gave them hope that land lay to the south. Navigating only by the currents and stars they sailed against the wind into the unknown expanse of blue. There, like the kuaka, they discovered a lonely land apart, a land of birds, of lush forest sanctuaries of ancient trees and hidden waterfalls, a land of plunging cliffs, wind swept coasts, gentle dunes and snow crowned mountains. They named it Aotearoa, the land of the long white cloud.

Almost a thousand years have past since man first reached these distant islands, and the kuaka still come to replenish themselves on our shores. Like the kuaka, man has discovered the wisdom in rest, the replenishment of body and soul. Ihu (pronounced e-who, meaning "to rest" in Maori) provides an escape from the pace and rush of everyday life. Luxury accommodation where you can stop, rest and experience the rare natural beauty of Aotearoa. Whether for a weekend, or a month, you will not leave unchanged.

172 (5ᵗʰ) logo for Kru Khmer | Design Firm: Graphaus, Astoria | Creative Director: Yuko Nakajima | Client: Kru Khmer

Description: Kru Khmer is a new spa brand based in Cambodia. Their products, such as bath salt and bath tea, are sold in stores throughout the city called Shiem Reap, where it's famous for Angkor Wat, Cambodia's biggest tourism site. Kru Khmer means "memtor" (in herbs and medical related matters) in Cambodian / Khmer language.

Kru Khmer was created to produce the very first made-in-Cambodia spa lines that are natural and high-end, for many tourists coming to Cambodia. Surprisingly there are almost no original high-end gift ideas coming out of in Cambodia. Many good products are imported from Thailand and if there is a product of Cambodian origin, they lack in design trends. They use natural herbs and ingredients from Cambodia, they hire Cambodian people, especially homeless, refugees and women from poor villages, who are treated like slaves in their hometowns.

Kru Khmer will lead a revolution in Cambodia, where people still fight for human rights and struggle to live as ordinary human beings. In this country people are not used to working for living because they highly depend on free resources from NGO organizations, and this company strives to teach people how to fish for themselves, rather than just handing out the fish to them. They create jobs for the local Cambodian people who have never had chances to work, and they are taught how to work for living in fare-trade concept.

173 PLATINUM Hanke Construction Logo | Design Firm: TOKY Branding + Design, St. Louis | Creative Director: Eric Thoelke | Designer: Travis Brown | Client: Hanke Construction

Description: Logo for a construction company.

174 South By Southwest Identity Family | Design Firm: Sibley Peteet Design Austin | Associate Creative Director: Susan Birkenmayer | Designer: Matthew Wetzler | Client: South By Southwest

Description: With the blurring of the lines between the three conferences increasing every year, they wanted to ensure that the family of identities embraced this convergence more so than in years past. This goal, in conjunction with 2010 being a year tied to science-fiction myth, led us to create a series of unique robots with interchangeable features that could be repurposed for a comprehensive modular system of identities. Besides, with the exception of John Connor, who doesn't like robots?

175 (1ˢᵗ) ExpoTurf Logo | Design Firm: Concussion LLP, Fort Worth | Chief Creative Officer: Andrew Yañez | Client: ExpoTurf

Credits&Comments

175 (2nd) Logo | Design Firm: RLR Advertising & Marketing, Pasadena | Designer: Thomas Rossman | Client: Bikewerks

Description: Bikewerks is a business-to-business bicycle service and maintenance company. They provide a range of both unique and standard bike services. These services are marketed to bicycle shops, department store bicycle departments and government agencies and companies with bicycle fleets. The bicycling community is about a more people and environmentally friendly approach to transportation. The logo's obvious nod to the Russian Constructivist posters of the 1930s is a reflection of this philosophy.

175 (3rd) Alta Torre | Design Firm: ARGUS, LLC, San Francisco | Creative Director: Jeff Breidenbach | Designer: Wilfred Castillo | Client: BRIDGE Housing Corporation

Description: ARGUS, LLC worked with BRIDGE Housing in the branding of their affordable housing project for senior citizens in Palo Alto, CA. The Alta Torre logo illustrates the contrast of the modern structure with lush, vegetative surroundings.

175 (4th) Angels & Cowboys logo/coaster | Design Firm: Michael Schwab Studio, San Anselmo | Illustrator: Michael Schwab | Client: Angels & Cowboys, Inc

Description: The logo for Angels & Cowboys Inc., the corporate creative partnership of graphic artist, Michael Schwab and photographer Kathryn Kleinman, is produced here as a coaster.

175 (5th) Snagdragon Logo | Design Firm: Siegel+Gale, New York | Creative Director: Matthias Mencke | Client: Qualcomm

176 City of Melbourne | Design Firm: Landor Associates, New York | Art Director, Creative Director: Jason Little | Creative Strategists: Katie Crosby, Cable Daniel-Dreyfus | Designers: Malin Holmstrom, Jefton Sungkar | Project Manager: Amanda Lawson | Senior Designers: Ivana Martinovic, Sam Pemberton | Strategy Director: James Cockerille | Client: City of Melbourne

Description: Melbourne is a dynamic and progressive city, internationally recognized for its diversity, innovation, sustainability and liveability. Our challenge was to create a new identity for the City of Melbourne that would reflect Melbourne's cool sophistication, capture the passion of the council and the people, and enable a unified and future focus for the City. In the 15 years since implementing its previous identity City of Melbourne had experienced significant change. As a result the organisation had accumulated a range of isolated logos for its various individual council services and these had become increasingly difficult and costly to manage. The fragmentation of this identity meant that equity was being driven away from the core brand and a long-term solution, rather than short-term fix, was required. Centred around a geometric framework, the new identity is as iconic and multi-faceted as the city itself. This framework allows for creative interpretation. At its heart, the M provides an iconic surface for endless visual executions to take place, adapting to suit the full range of services, initiatives and audiences.

177 Library Trucks Campaign | Design Firm: Barkley, Kansas City | Art Director: Glendon Scott | Creative Director: Tom Demetriou | Designer, Illustrator: Travis Kramer | Executive Creative Director: Brian Brooker | Client: Johnson County Library

MusicCDs

178 Everything That Happens Will Happen Today | Design Firm: Sagmeister, Inc. | Creative Director: Stefan Sagmeister | Designers: Joe Shouldice, Jared Stone, Richard The | Illustrator: Stephan Walter | Client: David Byrne & Brian Eno

Description: David Byrne and Brian Eno latest collaboration "Everything that Happens Will Happen Today" is exuberant and positive but reveals after several listenings a darker edge. We let this influence the design of the package. An idyllic suburban house sets the stage for many different scenes, from the seemingly innocuous (an oil stain on the driveway), to the curious (an industrial-size air conditioning unit on the front lawn) and the disturbing (a gasoline canteen in the kitchen)... All of them alluding to a deeper story which ultimately goes untold.

The special edition package features a miniature 3D diorama, light-activated sound-effects originating from within the house, a 92-page lyrics mini-booklet, the music CD, a bonus DVD with enhanced content as well as a pharmaceutical pill of uncertain content.

179 (1st) Sonic Boom | Design Firm: Michael Doret/Alphabet Soup Type Founders, Hollywood | Art Director: Paul Stanley | Artist, Designer: Michael Doret | Client: Simstan Music, Ltd.

Description: The assignment was to create a cover that was reminiscent of an earlier cover I had done for them—"Rock and Roll Over"—without it being a carbon copy. The rationale was that the group wanted the new album to be one which revisited their '70s roots as exemplified by the music on "Rock and Roll Over," and by its cover which many considered to have become iconic. They wanted to get back to the basic rock and roll which had made them famous, and they'd be recording using vintage equipment. They wanted the new cover to be reflective of that and to somehow hearken back to the earlier cover, the two designs perhaps acting as bookends for their career. Other than these parameters, and the fact that I needed to incorporate photographic representations of the four members, I had free reign to create the art as I saw fit. I decided that I'd turn the older design inside out, making the main element the somewhat explosive title lettering.

179 (2nd, 4th) New Zealand New Music CD Series 2009 - Volume XIV | Design Firm: Alt Group, Auckland | Creative Director: Dean Poole | Designers: Jinki Cambronero, Aaron Edwards, Tony Proffit, Shabnam Shiwan | Photographer: Toaki Okano | Client: New Zealand Trade & Enterprise

Description: A CD release to promote New Zealand music to decision makers in the international music industries. The package is sent to screen industry people that receive hundreds of CDs a week. It must be something they want to keep, but also fit into their existing CD archives. The intent is to create a memorable experience that is unique and visually arresting that then leads to an equally arresting aural experience. The cover references New Zealand's native songbird the Tui, through a surrealist lens.

The project was designing and physically building a sculpture for the cover image. It is built with reference to the vocabulary of forms found in surrealism—bones, props, birds, eggs and melting forms. The sculpture has a distinctive style in the realm between figuration and abstraction. The forms allude to organic life, but a fantastic sort that is found in natural history museums. Each package was sent to industry decision makers and includes a specially designed brooch that references elements in the CD cover composition—branch, egg, beak etc.

Each part was hand made using materials ranging from custom brass fittings to leather and wax. The skull was digitally modelled then rapid prototyped. The idea of an expansive colour field, without a horizon line represents the Surrealist concept of the "Marvellous" and is a metaphor for the subconscious realm of dreams.

179 (3rd) Eat your beats | Design Firm: Mangos, Malvern | Art Director, Illustrator: Jane Gast | Chief Creative Officer: Bradley Gast | Print Producer: Susan Trickel | Client: Maxfield Gast

Description: The illustration for "Eat Your Beats" has been designed to capture the essence of the music on the CD. The musician has layered multiple tracks and melodies, creating a cornucopia of sound that delights, and sometimes surprises, the listener. The goal was to capture this celebration of sound and rhythm graphically in a way that invites sharing the audio experience. The movement from black and white to the brightest of colors underscores the simplicity, complexity and multiple textures that make up the compositions.

Outdoor

180 Loose-Leaf Paper Bike-Rack | Design Firm: KNARF, New York | Art Director, Writer: Jelani Curtis William Wang | Creative Directors: Richard Wilde, Jeseok Yi | Executive Creative Director: Frank Anselmo | Client: School of Visual Arts

Description: Passers-by are inspired to see the world from a different perspective to remind them that creativity can happen anywhere and everywhere. Loose-leaf notebook pages made of heavy-duty 3M anti-slip vinyl were affixed on sidewalks beneath bike-racks.

181 Push The Envelope | Design Firm: KNARF, New York | Art Director, Designer, Writer: Frank Anselmo, Jayson Atienza | Creative Director: Jayson Atienza, Richard Wilde | Executive Creative Director: Frank Anselmo | Photographer: Billy Siegrist | Client: School of Visual Arts

Description: "Push The Envelope" is an American phrase which means to innovate, or go beyond commonly accepted boundaries. With this poster, The School of Visual Arts students literally "Pushed The Envelope."

Packaging

182 New Moon Promotional Mailer | Design Firm: Pitch, Culver City | Creative Director: Kim Thomsen | Designer: Gregory Bevington | Client: Burger King

Description: The creative objective behind innovating this sleek new standard of packaging was to bring these original The Twilight Saga: New Moon water bottles to life in a truly captivating way. Promoting efficiency, effectiveness and functionality, the double-sided promotional encasement with magnetic closure showcases the Team Edward and Team Jacob bottles together in one package, yet on opposing sides, playing on the team tension inherent in the property.

183 Soaps and Lotions Program | Design Firm: Michael Osborne, San Francisco | Art Director: Michael Osborne | Designers: Alice Koswara, Sheri Kuniyuki | Client: Williams-Sonoma

Description: Soaps and lotions program for Williams-Sonoma reflecting the brand's upscale and refined character.

184 Maybe It's Water | Design Firm: Bailey Lauerman, Lincoln | Art Directors: Ron Sack, James Strange | Creative Director: Carter Weitz | Client: Bootlegger, Inc.

Description: Water bottle packaging for Bootlegger, Inc., a liquor store.

185 Domingo's | Design Firm: Mark Oliver, Inc., Solvang | Creative Director: Mark Oliver | Designer: Patty Driskel | Typographer: John Burns | Client: Gaytan Food

186 EIRO Research Packaging | Design Firm: Pentagram Design, Austin | Art Director: DJ Stout | Client: EIRO Research

Description: Packaging for EIRO Research for high energy and vitamin juice drink.

187 O'Grady Olive Oil packaging | Design Firm: MacLaren McCann Calgary, Calgary | Art Director, Designer: Mark Lovely | Creative Director: Mike Meadus | Photographer: Justen Lacoursiere | Client: O'Grady Olive Oil

188 Fire Road Wines | Design Firm: The Creative Method, Surry Hills | Creative Director: Tony Ibbotson | Designer: Mayra Monobe | Client: Marlborough Valley Wines

Description: Re-design an existing range of labels creating a more simplified and contemporary solution. The labels origins are based on a famous fire in the Marlborough region that was bravely fought by local residents on a street now known as Fireroad. The designs needed to be bold, impact-full and driven by colour and story. There are currently 3 wines in the series but the designs must allow for additions to be added over the coming years.

189 Marlborough Sun Wines | Design Firm: The Creative Method, Surry Hills | Creative Director: Tony Ibbotson | Designer: Andi Yanto | Client: Marlborough Valley Wines

Description: To create a new series of wine labels from scratch. This is to include naming, identity and label design. The name and label needed to take advantage of the high profile of Marlborough wines across the globe. It needed to have a clear point of difference from other labels, as well as needing to standout on shelf, have a sense of humour and most importantly create a talking point. If there was a way that the labels could re-invent themselves each year this would also be an advantage as the grapes were specifically selected for each variety and need to display individual characteristics.

190 Carchelo Family | Design Firm: Eduardo del Fraile, Murcia | Designer: Eduardo del Fraile | Client: Carchelo

Description: Bodegas Carchelo is the first winery with guarantee of origin and quality of wines from Jumilla. The Monastrel and Syrah grapes with which the wine is made have a dry and very intense flavour. The client sought for a solid and outstanding label that would be unmistakable when looking at the bottles. The front of the labels mainly focuses on the initial of the type of wine and there is a photo which relates to the quality of its flavour. Carchelo, in spite of being a young wine, makes tears appear in the glass. There was the possibility of launching a message. Different sentences were chosen for each type of wine that would illustrate the ritual involved in wine tasting.

191 Pittyvaich 20-Year Old | Design Firm: The Brand Union, London | Designers: Glen Tutssel, Lauren Tutssel | Executive Creative Director: Glenn Tutssel | Client: Diageo

Description: Every year, Diageo produces a range of special releases selected from very rare or now closed distilleries. This year, the premium spirits house introduced three more to its range, one of which was the Pittyvaich 20-Year Old. A boxed whisky produced in very limited quantities, it retails for £200. We were tasked with designing a look and feel consistent with the Special Releases selection but with a bespoke visual identity befitting of its character and the benefit of the distillery. Pittyvaich's style is entirely typographic, extracted from the provenance of the distillery's rich heritage of journals, labels and certificates.

192, 193 PLATINUM Mannochmore 18-year old | Design Firm: The Brand Union, London | Designers: Glen Tutssel, Lauren Tutssel | Executive Creative Director: Glenn Tutssel | Illustrators: Andrew Davidson, Colin Frewin | Client: Diageo

Description: Every year, Diageo produces a range of special releases selected from very rare or now closed distilleries. This year, the premium spirits house introduced three more to its range, one of which was the Mannochmore 18-Year Old. A boxed whisky produced in very limited quantities, it retails for £200. We were tasked with designing a look and feel consistent with the Special Releases selection but with a bespoke visual identity befitting of its character and the benefit of the distillery. For Mannochmore, we looked to its environment and incorporated the region's native greater spotted woodpecker. The 18 holes that perforate the box packaging refer to both the age of the spirit as well as the wood maturation this whisky undergoes.

194, 195 PLATINUM Linkwood 26-Year Old | Design Firm: The Brand Union, London | Designer, Executive Creative Director: Glenn Tutssel | Typographers: Anthony Clayton, Glenn Tutssel | Client: Diageo

Description: Released as a range of three, Linkwood is a special release Speyside single malt Scotch whisky, bottled at natural cask strength. Diageo sought a design reflective of the rare whisky's heritage, provenance and preciousness, while conveying the unique flavouring of its special production.
The design took its cues from the special location of the original Linkwood distillery. A generation of swans still glide across the "Linkwood" distillery pond, where a timeless calm pervades the air around the old warehouses. Linkwood uses exact replicas of the original large stills to preserve every nuance of its delicate character.
Each pack's colour represents the type of barrel finish--each matured either in red wine, port or sherry casks. The typography is inspired by the distillery's original character and set in metal to give it authenticity. Specially commissioned engraved illustrations of the swans enhance provenance and appear in different modes of flight throughout the packaging.
At £250 a bottle, Linkwood was completely sold out before it was released.

196 PLATINUM The Managers Choice Single Cask Selection | Design Firm: The Brand Union, London | Designers: Glenn Tutssel, Lauren Tutssel | Executive Creative Director: Glenn Tutssel | Illustrators: Colin Frewin, James Frewin | Client: Diageo

Description: The Single Cask range from Diageo is a unique collection of 27 fine whiskies, each selected from Diageo's distilleries. These very rare whiskies are drawn from a single cask, each bottle is uniquely numbered and only a small number of bottles are produced.
Very special, these representative whiskies showcase the depth, breadth and variety of Diageo's offer of Scottish spirits. The challenge was to pull together these vastly different whiskies in flavour and personality, each retaining their sense of individuality and provenance, but marrying together under the mantle of "The Managers Choice" as one range. Unified by the same deep rich burgundy colour and range identity, each bottle incorporates individual iconography unique to each distillery. For example, Talisker's bottle is stamped with its trademark compass symbol, while Glen Elgin incorporates the iconic house martin into its design. A set typographic styling was used, overprinted with the relevant mandatory detail.
Of various ages, the whiskies retail from £150 plus per bottle and cater to the sophisticated tastes of connoisseurs, selling in Duty Free and select specialist whisky shops.

197 PLATINUM Benrinnes 23-Year Old | Design Firm: The Brand Union, London | Designers: Glenn Tutssel, Lauren Tutssel | Executive Creative Director: Glenn Tutssel | Illustrators: Andrew Davidson, Colin Frewin | Client: Diageo

Description: Every year, Diageo produces a range of special releases selected from very rare or now closed distilleries. This year, the premium spirits house introduced three more to its range, one of which was the Benrinnes 23-Year Old. A boxed whisky produced in very limited quantities, it retails for £200. We were tasked with designing a look and feel consistent with the Special Releases selection but with a bespoke visual identity befitting of its character and the benefit of the distillery. Benrinnes draws on the terrain of the area's beautiful heather-adorned landscape and endemic grouse bird, with a specially commissioned wood engraving.

198 Handle Your Business | Design Firm: McKinney, Durham | Account Director: Katie Clark | Art Director, Designer: Scott Pridgen | Chief Creative Officer: Jonathan Cude | Executive Creative Director: David Baldwin | Photographer: Stacy Evans | Print Producer: Lisa Kirkpatrick | Project Manager: Amy Norman | Writer: Brian Murray | Client: Big Boss Brewery

Description: How do you create beer packaging? Well, start with some beer. Add some WW II bomber names, random trivia, more beer, some gasket seals, a little bit of Spanish, a touch of German, more beer, a few pinup girls, a little bit of luck, more beer, swizzle sticks, mongrel dogs, fairy dust, a dash of kustom kulture, a heavy dose of metallic inks and some more beer. Stir. Serve cold.

199 Shiner Blonde Packaging | Design Firm: McGarrah Jessee, Austin | Creative Director: David Kampa | Designer: Erica Ellis | Writer: Tannen Campbell | Client: Spoetzl Brewery

Description: The assignment was to redesign Shiner Blonde packaging to better fit in with the other brews in its family. A Classic-Style Golden Lager, we wanted the packaging to reflect the timeless taste of the beer. As for the messaging on the beer, Shiner Blonde happens to be the local favorite in the town of Shiner, Texas, so we wanted to share that little nugget as well.

Posters

200 ReInvent | Design Firm: Vanderbyl Design, San Francisco | Art Director, Illustrator: Michael Vanderbyl | Designers: Kellie McCool, Michael Vanderbyl | Client: The Western Gallery, Western Washington University

Description: Poster for design exhibition.

201 PLATINUM "Another Japan" poster | Design Firm: Ichiro Watanabe Graphics, Osaka | Art Director, Designer: Ichiro Watanabe | Photographer: Toshiyuki Kuroishi | Client: Japan Graphic Designers Association (JAGDA)

Description: Traditional Japanese lacquer bowl, steam comes out and forms brilliant colors. I wanted to express that we in Asia are deeply connected. This was my work I entered for the exhibition "Another Japan" organized by JAGDA OSAKA.

202 2009 San Francisco Jewish Film Festival poster | Design Firm: Volume Inc., San Francisco | Art Directors: Adam Brodsley, Eric Heiman | Designer: Eric Heiman | Client: San Francisco Jewish Film Festival

Description: The 2009 San Francisco Jewish Film Festival campaign speaks to a contemporary Jewish culture that encompasses a more diverse range of experiences as Jews become more assimilated and, paradoxically, more "hidden in plain sight" amidst the ethnic melting pot of the Bay Area. Thus events like this film festival are when Jews and Judaism "emerge" (much like the typography in the materials) from this multi-cultural mélange to celebrate their heritage more acutely and publicly.

203 Outsourced Humanity | Design Firm: Alt Group, Auckland | Creative Director: Dean Poole | Designers: Kris Lane, Max Lozach | Client: Alt Group

Description: The project, EyeSaw is an annual event that invites Australasian designers to create and install a piece of visual communication on the walls of Omnibus Lane in Sydney. Designers were invited to respond to the theme "Humanity/Equality." For this poster the response to the brief became the act of commissioning the image. Faris Arori, a 27 year old Ramallah resident leads a team of volunteers that will write a message on the wall dividing Palestine from Israel for anyone willing to donate 30 Euros. Risking their own safety they give participants a chance to express themselves while raising awareness of "the physical presence" of the wall. The message "I outsource my humanity" is both a description and commentary on the act of its creation.

204 Social Energy | Design Firm: SenseTeam, Shenzhen | Creative Director: Yiyang Hei | Designers: Yiyang Hei, Zhao Liu, Xiaomeng Wang | Client: The OCT Art & Design Gallery

Description: This is an environmental design for "Social Energy-Contemporary Communication Design from the Netherlands "(Shenzhen). The exhibition is located in The OCT Art & Design Gallery which is the first Chinese museum themed with advantaged design. The environmental design of "Social Energy" (Shenzhen) employs the characteristic of hexagon on the Art & Design Gallery's outer wall. Design and integrate the energy structure of a tiny molecule. Explain the process of energy accumulation with huge red, white and blue gas-filling devices, leading audiences to a sumptuous and unique design feast. The interior of the exhibition also employs the concept of molecule structure. The molecule structure appears at every entrance and is used by the library's desks and chairs.

205 DEW Action Sports Tour | Design Firm: Saatchi & Saatchi LA, Torrance | Account Director: Marisstella Marinkovic | Art Directors: Abe Cortes, Mike Czako | Art Producer: Angee Murray | Associate Director of Brand Integration: Jennifer Jay | Creative Director: Ryan Jacobs | Executive Creative Director: Mike McKay | Illustrator: Tavis Coburn | Print Producer: Rachel Dallas-Noble | Writer: Bob Fremgen | Client: Toyota Motor Sales U.S.A., Inc.

Description: To leverage Toyota's sponsorship of the 2009 Summer Dew Action Sports Tour, we were tasked with developing unique creative in order to reach high rates of youth participation and spectatorship. The goal was to foster an emotional connection by leading the youth surveyed to begin to see the Toyota brand as "being like me." Drawing inspiration from the look and feel of 1960's monster movies, the posters reinterpreted action sports portraying the athletes as larger than life figures amid epic battles. We employed Tavis Coburn to execute the illustrations, presenting Toyota as a credible, authentic and relevant brand to a young and aesthetically savvy audience. The posters were handed out to fans at the DEW tour for the Toyota sponsored athletes to sign.

206 UN DAY CONCERT 2009 | Design Firm: Graphic Design Studio / United Nations, New York | Chief Creative Officer: Ziad Alkadri | Senior Designer: Matias Delfino | Client: The United Nations / Outreach Division / Department of Public Information

Description: United Nations Day is observed annually, marked throughout the world by concerts, meetings, discussions and exhibits on the achievements and goals of the United Nations. As indicated by the theme, A Tribute to Peacekeeping, the concert celebrates the United Nations Day 2009 by using different art forms to focus on the achievements and importance of United Nations peacekeeping. The poster was designed by the Graphic Design Unit, Outreach Division, DPI, United Nations, New York. The poster design introduces the blue helmet of the Peacekeeping Operations' soldiers. The blue helmet outlines the sound hole of an acoustic guitar. The color blue is the official color of the United Nations flag. Musical performances by artists from a broad array of countries, oral presentations by public figures, and documentary film clips highlighting the faces and stories of the people in the field, will be used to pay homage to the Blue Helmets on the sixty-fourth anniversary of the establishment of the United Nations. Among the artists who will perform are John McLaughlin (United Kingdom) with the band Remember Shakti (India), Emmanual Jal (Sudan), Sister Fa (Senegal), Salman Ahmad (Pakistan), Harry Belafonte (United States), Angelique Kidjo (Benin), Lang Lang (China) and Colombian band Aterciopelados. The Master of Ceremonies will be Isha Sesay of CNN International. The event aims to create greater public awareness of the important mission performed by peacekeeping operations around the globe.

207 Iranian Dissent Poster | Design Firm: Morla Design, San Francisco | Art Director: Jennifer Morla | Designers: Jennifer Morla, Anita Sarrett | Client: SocialDesignZine

Description: Morla Design was one of a select number of international designers and artists asked to create a poster for SocialDesignZine to address freedom of speech protests regarding the outcome of the 2009 Iranian elections.

Products

208 Duracell Instant Charger | Design Firm: Stuart Karten Design | Designers: Stuart Karten, Eric Schmid, Dennis Schroeder, Don Stiff | Client: Duracell

Description: Part of the emerging portable power reserve industry, the Instant Charger functions as a spare battery, providing convenient power for cell phones, smart phones, PDAs, MP3 players, iPods, digital cameras, and hand-held games. The 1150 mAh Lithium-ion battery stores up to 35 hours of backup power for all devices with regular USB ports or mini-USB ports. The compact device fits easily in a purse or pocket, eliminating the necessity of traveling with tangled power cords or bulky charging devices. By giving users added power efficiency in a simple and portable device, the charger allows consumers the freedom to live beyond the grid. The Instant Charger has a polished and sophisticated aesthetic, with a sleek profile and glossy front casing. The design adapts Duracell's well-known visual elements, such as the black and copper color scheme, to a new generation of personal products that address consumers' evolving power needs.

209 Flip camera skins | Design Firm: Volume Inc., San Francisco | Art Directors: Adam Brodsley, Eric Heiman | Designers: Adam Brodsley, Clara Daguin, Eric Heiman, Annie Krambuhl, Talin Wadsworth | Client: Pure Digital

Description: Custom skins for the popular Flip DV cameras.

Promotions/PaperCompanies

210, 211 The Standard, Volume 3 | Design Firm: Studio Hinrichs, San Francisco | Creative Director: Kit Hinrichs | Paper Type: Sappi Fine Paper North America | Print Run: Classic Color | Project Manager: Adi Wise | Senior Designer: Belle How | Writer: Delphine Hirasuna | Client: Sappi Fine Paper

Description: In Issue Three of The Standard, an ongoing series of print publications produced for Sappi Fine Paper, Studio Hinrichs was asked to examine and showcase ways that varnish and coatings can be used as a design technique. Designed to serve as a comprehensive reference tool, Standard 3 demonstrates a full range of techniques, with instructive notes, price/complexity ratings, a glossary of important terms, and a paper finish comparison. The book features images (food, fashion, etc.) where such techniques would make a powerful impression and covers the gamut from simple to complex. High-end marketing and catalog producers can gain tips on how to make their product so real that viewers can feel its texture and, in the case of some food products, smell its tantalizing aroma. "Varnish and Coatings" is the third book in The Standard series produced by Hinrichs and team. The other two were on "Prepress: Preparing Files for Print" and "Color Management."

212 Cougar, For a Great Performance | Design Firm: Squires & Company, Dallas | Creative Director: Laura Root | Designer: Michael Beukema | Client: Domtar Paper Company

Description: This brochure was designed for Domtar Paper Company to promote their most popular line of paper, Cougar. The piece directly compares Cougar's printability to that of its higher priced competitors, and the use of classic guitars as subject matter reinforces Cougar as a value sheet with reputation for beauty and reliability.

213 10401 | Design Firm: VSA Partners, Inc, Chicago | Account Director: Karolynn Earl | Creative Director: Dana Arnett | Designer: Michael Braley, Brandt Brinkerhoff | Writer: Jonathan Turitz | Client: Sappi Fine Paper North America

Promotions/Photographers

214, 215 Seven Assignments | Design Firm: Terry Vine Photography, Houston | Copywriter: Jolynn Rogers | Creative Director: Chris Hill | Designer: Bobby van Lenten | Photographer: Terry Vine | Printer: Blanchette Press | Client: Terry Vine Photography

Description: "Seven Assignments" is a collection of seven recent projects designed as individual books that are packaged in a small handmade wooden box. The boxed set is signed and numbered in a limited edition of 1,500 copies.

216, 217 Dinner Roles | Design Firm: Manarchy Films, Chicago | Art Director: Dennis Manarchy | Designer: Bill Sosin | Hair, Makeup: Cindy Adams | Print Producer: Andrea Walsh | Stylist: Mary Beth Manarchy | Client: Manarchy Films

Description: Dinner Roles is an exploration of period photography using antique cameras and conventional films. It has been a while since I used "film" so it was a bit confusing at first until I realized how beautiful analogue photography is. Dinner Roles recreates the looks of Kodachrome, wet plates, tintypes, and even the daguerreotype to some extent. It reenacts classic Americana scenes; Rosie the Riveter, the Spaghetti Girls, "Last Meal," Hopper's Diner, among others. It took a bit of work to research this project, but I must say it was a blast to do. It brought back a realization of the amazing quality of film.

Promotions/Printers

218, 219 PLATINUM What is the Story? | Design Firm: ARGUS, LLC, San Francisco | Creative Director: Jeff Breidenbach | Designer: Stephanie Wade | Photographer: Sven Wiederholt | Client: Fong & Fong Printers & Lithographers

Description: ARGUS, LLC worked with Fong & Fong, a Sacramento based full-service printer to produce a promotional piece which communicates the importance of the printed image and highlight special printing techniques. The brochure challenges the viewer to identify the stories shown individually on each spread. Printing techniques were integrated to help accentuate the visual dialogue and add impact. A production note insert acts as a key to the stories and how they were brought to life.

220 Brand Building Print | Design Firm: Bristol White, Las Vegas | Creative Director: Jeremy Bristol | Illustrators: Carl Medley, Jeff Wright | Photographer: Amber Gray | Print Producer: Arnie Feffer | Project Manager: Sally Miles | Strategy Director: Steve Theirault | Writer: Jill Beeler | Client: Quantum Group Printing

Description: Inspirational print capabilities brochure that takes the reader on an eight fold path to print enlightenment.

221 Gavin Martin's rabbit | Design Firm: Magpie Studio, London | Creative Directors: David Azurdia, Ben Christie, Jamie Ellul | Designers: Aimi Awang, Ben Christie, Tommy Taylor | Photographers: Paul Grundy, Murray Scott | Client: Gavin Martin Associates

Description: Award-winning printers Gavin Martin Associates wanted to promote their conversion to eco-friendly vegetable inks, whilst maintaining their commitment to the highest quality print.

We took them at their word, offering their customers "Unrivalled reproduction," and something to smile about in the process. Our giant rabbit—painstakingly created in carrots—not only formed a memorable image, but kept the local city farm in fodder for a week.

The oversized postal tube, bright orange and covered in mud, worked as an appropriate precursor to the main event.

Promotions/Retail

222 Gatorade Michael Jordan Limited Edition Media Kit | Design Firm: Fleishman-Hillard Creative, St. Louis | Designer: Louis Kokenis | Client: Gatorade

Description: Custom media kit announcing the introduction of Gatorade's limited edition Michael Jordan series. The kit included custom-designed packaging, flash drive, informational brochure, and samples of the product.

223 Chocolate press release | Design Firm: Colle + McVoy, Minneapolis | Art Director: Derek Till | Creative Director: Eric Husband | Design Director: Ed Bennett | Designer: Joe Monnens | Executive Creative Director: Mike Caguin | Writers: Emily Kaiden, Joel Stacy | Client: Caribou

Description: Instead of sending out a typical press release to promote how good Caribou Coffee's drinks made with all-natural Guittard chocolate are, we decided to craft our message out of the premium chocolate itself.

Stamps

224 PLATINUM (left) Bixby Bridge | Art Director: Carl T. Herrman | Artist: Dan Cosgrove | Client: United States Postal Service

224 PLATINUM (right) Mackinac Bridge | Art Director: Carl T. Herrman | Artist: Dan Cosgrove | Client: United States Postal Service

225 Cowboys of the Silver Screen | Art Director: Carl T. Herrman | Artist: Robert Rodriguez | Client: United States Postal Service

226 Abstract Expressionists | Art Director: Ethel Kessler | Client: United States Postal Service

227 (1st) Literary Arts: Julia de Burgos | Art Director: Howard E. Paine | Artist: Jody Hewgill | Client: United States Postal Service

227 (2nd) Black Heritage: Oscar Micheaux | Art Director: Derry Noyes | Artist: Gary Kelley | Client: United States Postal Service

227 (3rd) American Treasures: Winslow Homer | Art Director: Derry Noyes | Client: United States Postal Service

228 (top) Earth Hour | Design Firm: Hoyne Design, Victoria | Creative Director: Dan Johnson | Designer, Illustrator: Walter Ochoa | Client: Australia Post

Description: This series of stamps designed for Australia Post promoted Earth Hour 2009 and focused on three simple actions: turning lights out, switching power points off and saving energy (by unplugging). The two local stamps featured illustrations of nocturnal animals to highlight the "lights out" message. The international stamp included an Orang-utan, a species endangered by humanity's cavalier approach to the environment. The muted colour palette with cheerful colour highlights, reinforced the "lights out" message in a subtle way. The general public responded in a very positive way to the embedded messaging and playful tone. The stamps raised awareness of Earth Hour and encouraged involvement in a positive way.

228 (bottom) Justices of the Supreme Court of the United States | Art Director: Ethel Kessler | Designers: Rodolfo Castro, Lisa Catalone-Castro | Illustrator: Lisa Catalone-Castro | Client: United States Postal Service

229 (1st) Negro Leagues Baseball | Artist: Kadir Nelson | Art Director: Howard E. Paine | Client: United States Postal Service

229 (2nd) King and Queen of Hearts | Art Director, Designer, Typographer: Derry Noyes | Artist: Jeanne Greco | Client: United States Postal Service

229 (3rd) Abraham Lincoln | Art Director, Designer, Typographer: Richard Sheaff | Artist: Mark Summers | Client: United States Postal Service

Typography

230, 231 Lush Fashion & Art Magazine | Design Firm: Lush | Art Director, Designer, Typographer: Paul Sych | Client: Lush Fashion & Art Magazine

232, 233 Seeds of the Cities | Design Firm: SenseTeam, Shenzhen | Creative Director: Yiyang Hei | Designers: Yiyang Hei, Junrong Li, Jun Peng, Wei Yuan | Client: HSA

Description: "Seeds of the Cities": This is the Visual Identity System for Huasen Architecture Company's touring exhibitions. Perforated characters on the Visual Identity System are from the LED Indicating System of the exhibitions. Characters on the LED screen are made up of and shown by dots. They can change in any time. No matter c Characters, symbols or design are expressed through dots. Every exhibition area employs dynamic LED to show its Indicating System because we design a new kind of LED character for this Visual Identity System which will be used on LOGO, posters, books, invitations and hand bags. LED character shows texture through punching holes. Meanwhile, LED characters are circling from right to left. So, we design posters that are one relating to the other to symbolize the city's endless extension.

234 Polytrade Diary 2010 | Design Firm: Eric Chan Design Co. Ltd., Causeway Bay | Art Directors: Eric Chan, Iris Yu | Creative Director: Eric Chan | Designers: Claudia But, Manson Chan, Jim Wong, Iris Yu | Client: Polytrade Paper Corporation Limited

WinnersDirectory

3 Advertising www.whois3.com
1550 Mercantile Avenue NE, Second Floor
Albuquerque, NM 87107, United States
Tel 505 293 2333 | Fax 505 293 1198

601bisang www.601bisang.com
481-11 Seogyo-dong, Mapo-gu
Seoul, 121-839, Republic of Korea
Tel +82 2 332 2601 | Fax +82 2 332 2602

Addison www.addison.com
20 Exchange Place, 9th Floor
New York, NY10005, United States
Tel 212 229 5000 | Fax 212 929 3010

Alt Group www.altgroup.net
PO Box 47873, Ponsonby
Auckland 1144, New Zealand
Tel +64 9 360 3910

ando bv www.ando.eu
Mercuriusweg 37
2516 AW Den Haag, Netherlands
Tel +070 385 07 08 | Fax +070 385 07 09

ARGUS, LLC www.argussf.com
531 Howard Street, 2nd Floor
San Francisco, CA 94105, United States
Tel 415 247 2800 | Fax 415 247 2803

Arthur Steen Horne Adamson
www.ashawebsite.co.uk
Suite 404, Eagle Tower, Montpellier Drive
Cheltenham GL50 1TA, United Kingdom
Tel +01242 574 111

Bailey Lauerman www.baileylauerman.com
1248 O Street, Suite 900
Lincoln, NE 68508, United States
Tel 402 475 2800 | Fax 402 475 5115

Barkley www.barkleyus.com
1740 Main Street
Kansas City, MO 64108, United States
Tel 816 842 1500

Boccalatte www.boccalatte.com
507/55 Holt Street
Surry Hills, Sydney 2010, Australia
Tel +61 2 9211 9411

The Brand Union www.thebrandunion.com
11-33 St John Street
London EC1M 4AA, United Kingdom
Tel +44 0 207 559 7000 | Fax +44 0 207 559 7001

Bristol White www.bristolwhite.com
578 Brinkburn Point
Las Vegas, NV 89178, United States
Tel 702 217 7864

Butler, Shine, Stern & Partners www.bssp.com
20 Liberty Ship Way
Sausalito, CA 94965, United States
Tel 415 331 6049 | Fax 415 331 3524

Colle + McVoy www.collemcvoy.com
400 First Avenue North, Suite 700
Minneapolis, MN 55401, United States
Tel 612 305 6000 | Fax 612 305 6500

Concrete Design Communication
www.concrete.ca
2 Silver Avenue, 2nd Floor
Toronto, Ontario M6R 3A2, Canada
Tel 416 534 9960 | Fax 416 534 2184

Concussion LLP www.concussion.net
707 W Vickery Boulevard
Fort Worth, TX 76104, United States
Tel 817 336 6824

cottage industries
www.cottageindustriesdesign.com
2682 Glendal Boulevard
Los Angeles, CA 90039, United States
Tel 213 793 0987

The Creative Method
www.thecreativemethod.com
Studio 10, 50 Reservoir Street
Surry Hills, NSW 2010, Australia
Tel +61 2 82319977 | Fax +61 2 8231 9980

David Ferris Design www.davidferris.com
140 East 52nd Street, #6A
New York, NY 10022, United States
Tel 212 829 9352

David Sutherland Inc
679 Danielle Court
Rockwall, TX 75087, United States
Tel 214 638 4162

Design Army www.designarmy.com
510 H Sreet NE
Washington, DC 20002, United States
Tel 202 797 1018 | Fax 202 797 1807

Dominique Mousseau designer graphique
www.dmousseau.qc.ca
24, Avenue du Mont-Royal Ouest, #605
Montréal, Quebec H2T 2S2, Canada
Tel 514 845 6444

Eduardo del Fraile
www.eduardodelfraile.com
Saavedra Fajardo, 7, 2c
Murcia 30001, Spain
Tel +34 968 21 18 24 | Fax +34 968 21 80 87

Eric Chan Design Co. Ltd.
www.netvigator.com
Unit 601 6F Park Commercial Centre
180 Tung Lo Wan Road, Causeway Bay
Hong Kong
Tel +852 2527 7773 | Fax +852 2865 3929

fabrizio design
339 Aast 58 Street
New York, NY 10022, United States
Tel 212 308 5260

Faceout Studio www.faceoutstudio.com
520 SW Powerhouse Drive #628
Bend, OR 97702, United States
Tel 541 323 3220 | Fax 541 323 3221

fame-fame studio www.illinois.edu
408 East Peabody
Champaign, IL 61820, United States
Tel 217 244 5882

fd2s www.fd2s.com
500 Chicon, Austin, TX 78702, United States
Tel 512 476 7733

Ferreira Design Company
www.ferreiradesign.com
335 Stevens Creek Court
Alpharetta, GA 30005, United States
Tel 678 297 1903

Fleishman-Hillard Creative www.fleishman.com
200 North Broadway
St. Louis, MO 63102, United States
Tel 314 982 9149 | Fax 314 982 9144

frog design www.frogdesign.com
660 Third Street
San Francisco, CA 94107, United States
Tel 418 442 4804 | Fax 415 442 4803

gdloftPHL www.gdloft.com
1737 Wallace Street, Suite 201
Philadelphia, PA 19130, United States
Tel 267 761 9439

Gee + Chung Design www.geechungdesign.com
38 Bryant Street, Suite 100
San Francisco, CA 94105, United States
Tel 415 543 1192 | Fax 415 543 6088

Genesis, Inc. www.genesisinc.com
604 West 6th Avenue
Denver, CO 80204, United States
Tel 303 825 1230 | Fax 303 825 0096

Gensler www.gensler.com
2 Harrison Street, Suite 400
San Francisco, CA 94105, United States
Tel 415 433 3700 | Fax 415 836 4599

Goodby, Silverstein & Partners
www.goodbysilverstein.com
720 California Street
San Francisco, CA 94108, United States
Tel 415 392 0669 | Fax 415 788 4303

GQ www.condenast.com
4 Times Square Plaza, 9th Floor
New York, NY 10036, United States
Tel 212 286 6696 | Fax 212 286 8515

Graphic Design Studio / United Nations, New York
www.un.org, 00 East 42nd Street, Office IN-907c
New York, NY 10017, United States
Tel 212 963 2190

Graphaus www.graphaus.com
2523 31st Avenue, Apt 22
Astoria, NY 11106, United States
Tel 646 496 2174

GS Design www.gsdesign.com
6665 North Sidney Place
Milwaukee, WI 53213, United States
Tel 414 228 9666 | Fax 414 228 9652

Haas Design www.haasdesign.co.uk
9 Avenue Road, Eskbank
Edinburgh, Midlothian EH22 3BS, United Kingdom
Tel +44 131 660 3019

häfelinger+wagner design www.hwdesign.de
Türkenstraße 55 - 57
Munich, Bavaria 80799, Germany
Tel +0049 89 20 35 75 0 | Fax +0049 89 20 23 96 96

Hello Design www.hellodesign.com
8684 Washington Boulevard
Culver City, CA 90232, United States
Tel 310 839 4885 | Fax 310 839 4886

Hornall Anderson www.hadw.com
710 2nd Avenue, Suite 1300
Seattle, WA 98104, United States
Tel 206 826 2329 | Fax 206 467 6411

Hoyne Design www.hoyne.com.au
Level 1, 77a Acland Street
St Kilda, Victoria 3182, Australia
Tel +03 9537 1822 | Fax +03 9537 1833

Ichiro Watanabe Graphics
1-16 Nishitani Bldg., 1-10-11
Minamihorie, Nishi-ku, Osaka 550-0015, Japan
Tel +81 6 6532 0440

ico Design Consultancy Ltd
www.icodesign.co.uk
75-77 Great Portland Street
London W1W 7LR, United Kingdom
Tel +44 020 7323 1088

Infolio www.abcdesign.com.br
Rua Silveira Peixoto, 1040, cjto 1102
Curitiba, Paraná 80240-120, Brazil
Tel +55 41 3078 8050

Interbrand www.interbrand.com
130 Fifth Avenue, 4th Floor
New York, NY 10011, United States
Tel 212 798 7500 | Fax 212 798 7501

JohnstonWorks www.johnstonworks.com
Worlds End Studios
134 Lots Road, London
Greater London SW10 0RJ, United Kingdom
Tel +44 20 7349 7074

KMS TEAM www.kms-team.com
Tölzer Straße 2c, Munich 81379, Germany
Tel +49 89 490 411 0 | Fax +49 89 490 411 109

KNARF www.knarfny.com
10 West 15th Street #204
New York, NY 10011, United States
Tel 212 645 6277

Kym Abrams Design www.kad.com
213 West Institute Place, Suite 608
Chicago, IL 60610, United States
Tel 312 654 1005

Landor Associates www.landor.com
230 Park Avenue South, 6th Floor
New York, NY 10003, United States
Tel 212 614 4189

Lloyd & Company Advertising, Inc.
www.lloydandco.com
180 Varick Street, Suite 1018
New York, NY 10014, United States
Tel 212 414 3100 | Fax 212 414 3113

Lorenc+Yoo Design www.lorencyoodesign.com
109 Vickery Street
Roswell, GA 30075, United States
Tel 770 645-2828 | Fax 770 998-2452

Lush Fashion & Art Magazine www.lushmag.com
181 University Avenue, Suite 2010
Toronto, Ontario M5H 3M7, Canada
Tel 416 214 58997 | Fax 416 214 0525

MacLaren McCann Calgary www.maclaren.com
100, 238 11 Avenue SE
Calgary, Alberta T2G 0X8, Canada
Tel 403 269 6120 | Fax 403 263 4634

Magpie Studio www.magpie-studio.com
Hope House
12A Perseverance Works, 38 Kingsland Road
London E2 8DD, United Kingdom
Tel +020 7729 3007

Manarchy Films www.manarchy.com
656 West Hubbard Street
Chicago, IL 60654, United States
Tel 312 666 7400 | Fax 312 666 2400

Mangos www.mangosinc.com
10 Great Valley Parkway
Malvern, PA 19355, United States
Tel 610 296 2555 | Fax 610 640 9291

Mark Oliver, Inc. www.markoliverinc.com
984 Old Mission Drive, Suite A15
Solvang, CA 93463, United States
Tel 805 686 5166 | Fax 805 686 5224

Martin Williams www.martinwilliams.com
60 South Sixth Street, Suite 2800
Minneapolis, MN 55402, United States
Tel 612 340 0800 | Fax 612 342 9700

Matsumoto Inc. www.matsumotoinc.com
127 West 26th Streey, Suite 900
New York, NY 7626, United States
Tel 212 807 0248 | Fax 212 807 1527

Maud www.maud.com.au
Suite 3, Level 3, 2-12 Foveaux Street
Surry Hills, NSW 2010, Australia
Tel +61 2 9029 6497

McGarrah Jessee www.mc-j.com
205 Brazos, Austin, TX 78701, United States
Tel 512 225 2263 | Fax 512 225 2020

McKinney www.mckinney.com
318 Blackwell Street
Durham, NC 27701, United States
Tel 919 313 4125 | Fax 919 313 0805

McMillan Group www.mcmillangroup.com
25 Otter Trail
Westport, CT 06880, United States
Tel 203 227 8696 | Fax 203 227 2898

Metal www.revistametal.com
Aribau, 168 1° 1ª. 08036 Barcelona, Spain
Tel +34932955840

Methodologie www.methodologie.com
720 Third Avenue, Suite 800
Seattle, WA 98104-1870, United States
Tel 206 623 1044 | Fax 206 625 0154

Michael Doret/Alphabet Soup Type Founders
www.MichaelDoret.com
6545 Cahuenga Terrace
Hollywood, CA 90068, United States
Tel 323 467 1900

Michael Osborne www.modsf.com
444 De Haro Street, Suite 207
San Francisco, CA 94107, United States
Tel 415 255 0125 | Fax 415 255 1312

Michael Schwab Studio
www.michaelschwab.com
108 Tamalpais Avenue
San Anselmo, CA 94960, United States
Tel 415-257-5792 | Fax 415-257-5793

MiresBall, Inc. www.miresball.com
2345 Kettner Boulevard
San Diego, CA 92101, United States
Tel 619 234 6631

Mirko Ilic Corp www.mirkoilic.com
207 East 32nd Street, 4th Floor
New York, NY10016, United States
Tel 212 481 9737 | Fax 212 481 7088

mono www.mono-1.com
3036 Hennepin Avenue
Minneapolis, MN 55408, United States
Tel 612 454 4900

Morla Design www.morladesign.com
1008A Pennsylvania Avenue
San Francisco, CA 94107, United States
Tel 415 577 2023

Mytton Williams Ltd www.myttonwilliams.co.uk
1-4 Daniel Mews
Bath, Somerset BA2 6NG, United Kingdom
Tel + 44 0 1225 476 476 | Fax +44 0 1225 427 674

Nuts About Design
77 Beattie Street, Balmain, NSW 2041, Australia
Tel +02 9555 2466 | Fax +02 9555 2477

oakwood media group www.oakwood-dc.com
7 Park Street, Bristol BS1 5NF, United Kingdom
Tel +44 117 983 6789 | Fax +44 117 983 7323

Office www.visitoffice.com
1060 Capp Street
San Francisco, CA 94110, United States
Tel 415 447 9850 | Fax 415 447 9208

Penguin Group (USA) Inc.
www.us.penguingroup.com
375 Hudson Street, 3rd Floor
New York, NY 10014, United States
Tel 212 366 2176

Pentagram Design www.pentagram.com
1508 West 5th Street
Austin, TX 78703, United States
Tel 512 476 3076 | Fax 512 476 5725

Periscope www.periscope.com
921 Washington Avenue South
Minneapolis, MN 55415, United States
Tel 612 399 0500 | Fax 612 399 0600

Peter Kraemer www. peterkraemer-web.de
Lindemannstr. 31, Düsseldorf 40237, Germany
Tel +49 211 2108087 | Fax +49 211 228541

Philographica www.philographica.com
1318 Beacon Street, Suite 12
Brookline, MA 02446, United States
Tel 617 738 5800 | Fax 617 738 5889

Pitch www.thepitchagency.com
8825 National Boulevard
Culver City, CA 90232, United States
Tel 424 603 6030

pivot design, inc. www.pivotdesign.com
230 West Huron, 4th Floor
Chicago, IL 60610, United States
Tel 312 787 7707 | Fax 312 787 7737

POLLOCK
1519 21A Steet NW
Calgary, Alberta T2N 2M7, Canada
Tel 403 975 9495

Ralph Appelbaum Associates Inc www.raany.com
88 Pine Street 29th Floor
New York, NY 10005, United States
Tel 212 334 8200 | Fax 212 334 6214

RLR Advertising & Marketing
150 South Arroyo Parkway
Pasadena, CA 91105, United States
Tel 626 440 0321 | Fax 626 796 5634

Rosebud, Inc. www.rosebud-inc.com
Salmgasse 4a, Vienna 1030, Austria
Tel +43 1 535 49 70 14

Saatchi & Saatchi LA www.saatchila.com
3501 Sepulveda Boulevard
Torrance, CA 90503, United States
Tel 310 214 6000 | Fax 310 214 6160

Saatchi Design Worldwide www.saatchi.co.nz
PO Box 801, Auckland, New Zealand
Tel +64 9 355 5000 | Fax +64 9 355 1838

Sagmeister, Inc. www.sagmeister.com
206 West 23rd Street, 4th Floor
New York, NY 10011, United States
Tel 212 647 1789 | Fax 212 647 1788

SenseTeam www.sensebrand.com
15C Block B, City of Garden, Jintang Road
Shenzhen, Guangdong 518029, China
Tel +86 755 82484647

Shin Matsunaga Design Inc.
Shinjuku-ku, Yarai-cho, 98-4
Tokyo 162-0805, Japan
Tel +81 3 5225 0777 | Fax +81 3 3266 5600

Shine Advertising www.shinenorth.com
612 West Main Street #105
Madison, WI 53562, United States
Tel 608 442 7373 | Fax 608 442 7374

SHR Perceptual Management
www.shrbranding.com
6215 North 61st Street
Paradise Valley, AZ 85253, United States
Tel 480 483 3700 | Fax 480 483 9675

Sibley Peteet Design Austin www.spdaustin.com
522 East 6th Street
Austin, TX 78701, United States
Tel 512 473 2333 | Fax 512 473 2431

Siegel+Gale www.siegelgale.com
625 Avenue of the Americas, 4th Floor
New York, NY 10011, United States
Tel 212 453 0423 | Fax 646 514 1369

Squires & Company www.squirescompany.com
2913 Canton Street
Dallas, TX 75226, United States
Tel 214 939 9194 | Fax 214 939 3464

St. Martin's Press www.stmartins.com
175 Fifth Avenue, Suite 400
New York, NY 10010, United States
Tel 646 307 5100 | Fax 212 529 1540

Steven Taylor & Associates
The Plaza, Unit 3.17, 535 Kings Road
London SW10 0SZ, United Kingdom
Tel +0044 20 73512345

Stoltze Design www.stoltze.com
15 Channel Center Street, Unit 603
Boston, MA 02210, United States
Tel 617 350 7109 | Fax 617 482 1171

Stuart Karten Design www.kartendesign.com
4204 Glencoe Avenue
Marina del Rey, CA 90292, United States
Tel 310-827-8722

Studio Hinrichs www.studio-hinrichs.com
387 Tehama Street
San Francisco, CA 94103, United States
Tel 415 543 1776 | Fax 415 543 1775

STUDIO INTERNATIONAL
www.studio-international.com
Buconjićeva 43, Buconjićeva 43/III
Zagreb, HR-10 000, Croatia
Tel +385 1 37 40 404 | Fax +385 1 37 08 320

studio NEWWORK www.studionewwork.com
503 Grand Street, Apt#1
New York, NY 10002, United States
Tel 917 651 4437

SVIDesign www.svidesign.com
124 Westbourne Studios
242 Acklam Road
London W10 5JJ, United Kingdom
Tel +0 20 7524 7808

Terry Vine Photography www.terryvine.com
2417 Bartlett Street
Houston, TX 77098, United States
Tel 713 528 6788 | Fax 713 528 6852

Texas State University www.txstate.edu
1506 IH35 South #5312
San Marcos, TX 78666, United States
Tel 515 203 9430

thomas.matthews www.thomasmatthews.com
8 Disney Street, London SE1 1JF, United Kingdom
Tel +0207 403 4281 | Fax +0207 403 4268

TOKY Branding + Design www.toky.com
3001 Locust Street
St. Louis, MO 63103, United States
Tel 314 534 2000 | Fax 314 534 2001

Toolbox Design www.toolboxdesign.com
403-1228 Hamilton Street
Vancouver, British Columbia V6B 6L2, Canada
Tel 604 739 9932 | Fax 604 696 9973

Turner Duckworth www.turnerduckworth.com
831 Montgomery Street
San Francisco, CA 94133, United States
Tel 415 675 7777

Underline Studio www.underlinestudio.com
26 Soho Street, Suite 204
Toronto, Ontario M5V 1Z7, Canada
Tel 416 341 0475 | Fax 416 341 0945

Urban Influence www.urbaninfluence.com
3201 1st Avenue South, Suite 110
Seattle, WA 98134, United States
Tel 206 219 5599

Vanderbyl Design www.vanderbyldesign.com
171 2nd Street, 2nd Floor
San Francisco, CA 94105, United States
Tel 415 543 8447 | Fax 415 543 9058

VBAT www.vbat.com
Pilotenstraat 41A
Amsterdam 1059 CH, Netherlands
Tel +31 0 20 750 3000 | Fax +31 0 20 750 3001

Ventress Design Group, Inc. www.ventress.com
PO Box 158544
Nashville, TN 37215-5844, United States
Tel 615 727 0155

Visual Arts Press, Ltd. www.sva.edu
220 East 23rd Street, Suite 311
New York, NY 10010, United States
Tel 212 592 2380 | Fax 212 696 0552

Volume Inc. www.volumesf.com
2130 Harrison Street, Suite B
San Francisco, CA 94110, United States
Tel 415 503 0800 | Fax 415 503 0818

VSA Partners, Inc www.vsapartners.com
1347 South State Street
Chicago, IL 60605, United States
Tel 212 869 1188 | Fax 212 869 0099

Wall-to-Wall Studios www.walltowall.com
1010 Western Avenue, Suite 302
Pittsburgh, PA 15233, United States
Tel 412 232 0880 | Fax 412 232 0906

Wallace Church, Inc. www.wallacechurch.com
330 East 48th Street
New York, NY 10017, United States
Tel 212 755 2903 | Fax 212 355 6872

WAX www.waxpartnership.com
320 333 24 Avenue SW
Calgary, Alberta T2T 0J5, Canada
Tel 403 262 9323 | Fax 403 262 9399

Webster Design Associates
www.websterdesign.com
5060 Dodge Street, Suite 2000
Omaha, NE 68132, United States
Tel 402 551 0503 | Fax 402 551 1410

Yonalee Design
2841 34th Street
Astoria, NY 11103, United States
Tel 203 685 8101

Designers

ArtDirectors

Clients

CreativeDirectors

Illustrators

DesignFirms

ExecutiveCreativeDirectors

ProjectManagers

SeniorDesigners

WebDevelopers

Writers

Two ways to dramatically save on our Books!

Receive 30% off the retail price, or $50 for a $70 book, and
immediately get a free digital copy of the book, when you buy
Annuals directly from www.graphis.com.

Receive our best deal when you purchase a Graphis Professional
Membership for $120. You'll receive 40% off the retail price of
new Annuals, or $40 for a $70 book, plus immediately get a free
digital copy of the book, and you'll also save on Call-for-Entry
fees and other Graphis books.

Graphis Design Titles

Poster Annual 2011	Design Annual 2011	New Talent Annual 2010	Advertising 2011	Annual Reports 2010
Brochures 6	Letterhead 7	Logo 7	Product Design 3	Promotion Design 2
The Illustrated Voice	12 Japanese Masters	designing: Chermayeff & Geismar	Exhibition: The Work of Socio X	Masters of the 20th Century

"After the ideas in this book are stolen, at least we have documentation of the true originators."

Design Journal Americas 001

Please visit www.graphis.com for more information on each title.